# Enjoy
# retirement

# Enjoy
# retirement

### 52 brilliant ideas for
### loving life after work

## Janet Butwell

brilliant
ideas

## CAREFUL NOW

Some people seem to have come to the conclusion they can get compensation for just about anything that goes wrong in their lives these days, so forgive me for being a bit stroppy now. Whatever age you are life's about risk, and you don't get to be compensated for getting into some kind of trouble just because something you've done was sparked by an idea you read in this book. Your actions are your own responsibility and it's up to you to make sensible choices. The publishers and I are not prepared to accept any responsibility for any kind of harm or damage that comes to you from any decision you reach as a result of reading this book. If you're in any doubt about whether your ideas are safe, speak to an expert on the subject (if you're the litigious kind, find one who's got insurance cover). And don't do anything I wouldn't do.

Copyright © The Infinite Ideas Company Limited, 2006

The right of Janet Butwell to be identified as the author of this book has been asserted in accordance with the Copyright, Designs and Patents Act 1988.

First published in 2006 by
**The Infinite Ideas Company Limited**
36 St Giles
Oxford
OX1 3LD
United Kingdom
www.infideas.com

A CIP catalogue record for this book is available from the British Library.

ISBN 1-904902-58-8

Brand and product names are trademarks or registered trademarks of their respective owners.

Designed and typeset by Baseline Arts Ltd, Oxford
Printed by TJ International, Cornwall

# Brilliant ideas

**Brilliant features** .................................................................................. xiii

**Introduction** ........................................................................................ xiv

1. **Glory days** ..................................................................................... 1
   Find out how to live in the moment and make the days of your retirement your glory days.

2. **Book the bungee jump** ............................................................... 5
   There's a growing trend for pensioners to take up physically challenging sports. Well, why not? Let's see what gets your adrenalin pumping.

3. **Retire to work** ............................................................................. 9
   Jobs for the over fifties? You're having a laugh aren't you? There are more opportunities than there used to be, and with a little know-how you can track down a job that will suit you.

4. **Just get out from under my feet, will you?** ............................ 13
   Togetherness may be great for a weekend or a holiday, but it's not always so great when you and your partner are forced to share the same space full time. Anticipate problems and work out how to avoid them.

5. **Spend it like Beckham?** ............................................................. 17
   If you've always spent your income (or even more than your income) and you can't imagine how you'll cope on your pension, this one's for you. It's all about managing the budget.

6. **Use it or lose it** ...............................................................................21

What's all that down there made of? Muscle! What does muscle do if it isn't used? It withers. You're never too old for sex, so get flexing.

7. **Don't act your age** ...........................................................................25

Hey. This is going to be great. It'll be the first time since you were a child that you'll have the chance to have fun without feeling guilty. Can you even remember what fun is? Remind yourself of the things that make you laugh.

8. **The cry of the beholder** ...................................................................29

We've all heard the bitchy comments: 'Do you think he's wearing a toupee?' 'Look at her! Has she had another face lift?' Ignore the critics. Look good and be proud of yourself.

9. **From here to eternity** .......................................................................35

Some people think retirement's just one long holiday. But exactly what is a holiday for you? What makes it different from daily life? Have another look at your holiday plans before you settle for the usual comfort zone.

10. **Where there's a way...there's a will** ...............................................39

It can be a weight off your mind to know you've found a way to take care of your loved ones after you pop your clogs. Make sure now that they can manage after you're gone.

11. **Safety first?** ....................................................................................43

Are pensioners more vulnerable to crime than other people? Well, no, but if you're worried, do something to help yourself anyway.

12. **Chocolate is bad for you** ................................................................47

And so are cakes, biscuits, sweets...and diets. But obesity puts you in the risk zone for illness so don't ignore it. Bin the diet books and look at better ways of keeping your weight under control.

13. **The voice that whispers in your ear**.........................................................53
You know what I mean. That insidious inner demon that tells you 'You're not good enough.' Well the demon's had a good run but now's the time to get rid of it forever and boost your self-image.

14. **The march of age** ...................................................................................59
Take a look around you. See how our society treats pensioners. Do you want that to happen to you? Make a stand against ageist attitudes.

15. **Don't do it**............................................................................................63
Relax. De-stress. In fact, let's go a bit further than that and learn the art of meditation. You've got the time now, right?

16. **Earplugs at the ready?** ...........................................................................69
Because if action really does speak louder than words, you're about to make a lot of noise. Get started on those goals.

17. **Get the pasting table out of the attic** ....................................................73
It's not only the wrinkles on your face that age you. Give your home a facelift.

18. **Where's the Enigma machine when you need it?** ......................................77
Because if you haven't already found out, you'll soon discover when you get your pension forecast that it's in a kind of code. You may need to call in the experts.

19. **VO2 max it**...........................................................................................83
Whaddya mean you don't understand? Shame on you. Get down and work that body at once.

20. **Retired people are invisible** ...................................................................87
People tend to class anyone with lines on their face and a few grey hairs as 'just another old person'. Keep your personality intact. Walk the fine line between passivity and aggression and make sure you're not overlooked.

21. **Don't split hairs**......................................................................................91

Now you've left work you can relax on the grooming regime can't you? Well, no. Unkempt hair, torn nails and eau de tramp aren't nice. Have a long, hard look at yourself and make sure you're not displaying bag lady chic.

22. **Bingo, bowls and the church choir**..........................................................95

Community activities for the retired seem to have got stuck in a time warp. Can we invent something new? Or maybe it's already out there and no one's told us? Well, it's a bit of both actually.

23. **Only the lonely**.........................................................................................99

There's nothing sadder than someone struggling alone, unnoticed. Unless it's two lonely people living yards away from each other and never speaking. Build yourself a network of new friends.

24. **Stop swinging that poor cat**...................................................................105

There are better ways of working out how much space you need in your home now you're retired. In fact, there are probably better ways of using the space you've got.

25. **Chocolate is good for you**.......................................................................109

(Well, as long as it's not your staple diet.) Ditch the supplements and start to eat the kind of food your body really needs to keep it healthy.

26. **If you think you're stressed now...**.........................................................113

Retiring doesn't banish stress – it just brings a whole new lot of things to stress you out. This is bad news (especially at your age!) so when it happens you need to be able to manage it.

27. **A brand named 'old'**.................................................................................117

Teenagers are punks with multiple piercings one year, Goths with black eyeliner the next, and then elegant Romantics! But old people are always just old people. Why? Find out, and avoid becoming a stereotype.

28. **Doing the crossword isn't enough** ........................................................121
(Especially if it's in the same newspaper every day.) You want to stay sharp and alert till the day you die, so how many ways can you find to stretch your mind and keep those brain cells working?

29. **Eating the elephant** ...............................................................................127
Obviously, you do it one bite at a time, which is exactly how you deal with major problems.

30. **Kids' stuff** ............................................................................................131
Are your children still on your hands? Or are you on theirs? This one's about how to manage the changing relationship between you and your offspring once retirement is reality. Oh, you don't think it'll change? Just wait and see!

31. **Burn the pipe and slippers** ...................................................................135
Trust me. You don't want to spend your retirement sitting in an armchair watching TV when you can be having the best time of your life. Work out what gets you really excited.

32. **Try an alternative approach** ..................................................................139
Bad back? Try Alexander lessons or an aromatherapy massage. Stressed? What about tai chi or meditation? You're never too old to try alternative therapies, and you may be surprised how effective they can be.

33. **Feeling blue?** .......................................................................................143
Depression is one of the most common illnesses but it's sometimes difficult to spot. So first you have to recognise it; then you have to find enough energy to want to beat it. Learn how.

34. **Get into the closet** ................................................................................149
Why do so many people dress like old people? What's wrong with being stylish?

35. **Oh. The paint's all dried up** ..................................................................155
Take a fresh look at how you spend your leisure time and find some new interests.

36. **Who cares?** ...................................................................................................159

One way or another we're all caring for someone, and being cared for in return, but the day may come when this means more than the odd friendly hug, so be prepared.

37. **Planes, trains and free travel passes** ...................................................163

You may be looking forward to the end of commuting, but you'll still have to get around. Review your travel needs, especially if you live somewhere isolated.

38. **Balance the health budget**...................................................................167

There's no getting away from it. As we age we are more susceptible to certain illnesses. Still, there are ways of minimising the risks, so let me put you on the right track for a healthy, fit old age.

39. **Let's give it up for the wrinklies** ..........................................................173

You're still smoking? Alcohol consumption a bit excessive? Break the habit before your doctor starts putting the frighteners on. Try the one-nail-at-a-time approach.

40. **'I used to be someone, but now I'm retired'** ......................................177

If you thought it was bad telling people you were a dentist/right-wing despot/tax inspector, it's worse telling them you're retired. Find a way to describe yourself that will give you real status and won't trigger that glazed look of boredom in new acquaintances.

41. **Get an MOT** .....................................................................................181

No, silly. Not the car – you. Regular health checks really are worthwhile, believe me.

42. **Look back in anticipation**...................................................................185

How's it working for you so far? Is retirement everything you hoped for, or did you try a few things and then get stuck in an uncomfortable comfort zone? Why not call 'time out' to make a progress check?

43. **Who loves ya?** ................................................................189

You're probably beginning to realise that life's too short to fall out with people you love. Is it too late to put things right? Of course not. It just takes a bit of know-how (and some courage).

44. **Banks don't pay loyalty bonuses**........................................193

There are better ways to manage your investments than playing safe with the old deposit account. Make your savings earn more with a bit of research and some nifty footwork.

45. **From Apple to Zimmer**......................................................199

Life used to be grim – imagine being old in the fourteenth century. Then celebrate your luck by taking advantage of the great resources available today. From computers to walking aids there's almost certainly something out there to make your life better.

46. **Be needed, not needy** ......................................................203

It's horribly easy to lose your independence. It usually starts when you start relying on other people to do things you can do yourself. Take responsibility for yourself. Even better, take responsibility for someone else.

47. **Location, location, location**................................................207

A place in the country sounds great. But wait – you need shops, pubs, restaurants! And where's the local doctor's surgery, or the dentist? Before you downsize, give some thought to local facilities.

48. **Grandma Moses was seventy-five** ....................................211

Just because you've had a lot of birthdays doesn't mean you've run out of bright ideas. In fact, what you lack in youth and energy you'll make up for in enthusiasm and experience. Give some thought to what inspires you and get creative.

**49. Life after death** .................................................................................................215

Dealing with the death of a person you love is the hardest thing you'll ever have to do, but believe me you will deal with it and rebuild your life. There is life after death: yours, and piecing it back together is by far the best way you can honour the memory of someone who loved you.

**50. Lawn today, lawn tomorrow** ...........................................................................219

It'll still be there. Still needing cutting, raking, weeding, seeding and feeding. Are you a lifelong non-gardener? Do you have a field outside the front door? Plant the kind of garden that works for you.

**51. My arm isn't long enough** ...............................................................................225

If you can't hold the paper far enough away to be able to read it, you're already familiar with the joys of long-sightedness. Nature has lots of weird little surprises in store as all sorts of bits take turns to grumble, or simply go on strike. Here are few little tips for dealing with new-found physical limitations.

**52. First amongst equals** .....................................................................................229

Sometimes it's difficult to decide where your priorities lie, particularly if you're busy. Brush up your time management skills for a more enjoyable retirement.

**The End** .................................................................................................................234

Or is it a new beginning?

**Where it's at** ........................................................................................................236

Index

# Brilliant features

**Each chapter of this book is designed to provide you with an inspirational idea that you can read quickly and put into practice straight away.**

Throughout you'll find four features that will help you to get right to the heart of the idea:

- *Here's an idea for you* Take it on board and give it a go – right here, right now. Get an idea of how well you're doing so far.

- *Try another idea* If this idea looks like a life-changer then there's no time to lose. *Try another idea* will point you straight to a related tip to enhance and expand on the first.

- *Defining idea* Words of wisdom from masters and mistresses of the art, plus some interesting hangers-on.

- *How did it go?* If at first you do succeed, try to hide your amazement. If, on the other hand, you don't, then this is where you'll find a Q and A that highlights common problems and how to get over them.

# Introduction

*'Life belongs to the living, and he who lives must be prepared for changes.'*
JOHANN WOLFGANG VON GOETHE

Does the looming prospect of retirement frighten the life out of you? Or are you already retired and wondering why on earth everyone's treating you as if you were ancient, even though you know you're the same person you were when you were twenty?

Whether you're planning retirement or you're an old hand at being a pensioner, this book's for you. It's not like most retirement books. It doesn't imply you've handed over your wits in part-exchange for the pension book; nor does it believe that all that matters to you is the amount of pension you can get, how many holidays you can arrange this year, and where you can bulk-buy support hose. And, most of all, it doesn't assume that retirement's the end of your life, and that all you can do now is fill in the time as best as you can till you die.

OK, that's what it's not, but what is it? It's a book about change. It's about managing one of the biggest changes we ever face, and it's about continuing to change and adapt over the next decades of your life. It's about getting the most out of your life, no matter who you are and what your circumstances are, and it's about having fun.

The book's packed with ideas to get you thinking, and planning, and living life to the full. Obviously, I can't tell you how to live your retirement but, as someone who had a complete panic a couple of years back when I reached 55 and has been frantically researching the whole topic of 'being a pensioner' ever since, I reckon I've worked out what matters most. So this book's about how to explore your options and decide what you want from your life, and it's about all the things that might be a factor in your new life. You can dip into the ideas that seem most relevant to you, or you can start at page 1 and keep reading – or you can follow the links which, if I've got them right, will take you right through all 52 ideas.

This book's also a bit of a call to action, because in two years of research I've also worked out what irritates me most about 'retirement'. It's the image. I'm genuinely appalled at the majority of advice aimed at pensioners, and at the way society views anyone drawing a pension. It starts on the very day you hit that dreaded half-century. Along with the hilarious 'omigod you're 50' cards you find the first trickle of what turns into a daily deluge of junk mail. Specialist holidays for the elderly, cheap insurance deals (because you're going to pop your clogs any minute), warden-controlled accommodation – what are they thinking of?

We've all seen the comments about 30-year-old sportsmen being 'over the hill' but it comes as a genuine surprise to find that some people really do believe that retirement is the end of real life. Yet we're fitter and healthier than our parents' generation and – whatever the world thinks – we're looking forward to many years of active life. In fact, let's just get this clear right now.

To my generation (the real Baby Boomers, born after the end of the Second World War) the traditional picture of old age is anathema. We're used to having the world revolve around us and we don't see why that should stop just because we've reached retirement age. We are, after all, the rock 'n' roll generation; the generation who lit up the 60s and made the 70s so outrageous. *We* can't possibly be *old*.

So as you read through the 52 ideas you're going to learn to stand up for yourself and you're going to be taking a good hard look at your life. Are you healthy, fit and happy? What problems do you have? Which of them can be solved? Which can't? What future do you have in mind? Is it what you really want? Give yourself the luxury of a week of navel gazing to decide exactly what you want from your future!

# 1

# Glory days

**Find out how to live in the moment and make the days of your retirement your glory days.**

Have you noticed that some retired people talk endlessly about the past? My theory is that it's because they don't have a present!

Don't misunderstand me. I'm not suggesting there's anything wrong in talking about the past (with people who genuinely want to hear about it). And there's nothing wrong in recalling great memories – they are, after all, the things that have made you who you are. But you don't want to spend your whole time savouring past joys so that you can ignore a dull present. Do you ever do this?

Well, have you ever interrupted an urgent discussion with an irrelevant story? (For example when your music-loving grandchildren had some cash to spend and were arguing about the relative merits of Blue Bunnie and The Suede Carpets and you joined the conversation with 'When I was your age I remember buying Blue Suede Shoes. Now there was a great singer…'). If you've done this, stop and think about why you did it. Was it because you thought your memories would help their decision? Or was it because you weren't really sure who they were talking about so you found you couldn't contribute in any other way to their conversation?

*Here's an idea for you...* **Why not write about the things you love thinking about? Things you've experienced in the past and believe other people will be interested in. This really is living in the moment – you'll have to give total concentration to the craft of writing and you'll become lost in the task.**

Conversely, have you ever turned the wrong way down a one-way street because you were concentrating so hard on what you were going to do when you arrived at your destination that you forgot to look where you were going? Or bumped into someone at the station because you were so focused on the almost-closed train doors?

Watch a cat, blissfully enjoying a small patch of sun on a cold day. It knows what *carpe diem* means. But humans seem congenitally incapable of seizing the day. As children we're desperate to grow up, and as adults we're either thinking about tomorrow's problems, planning our next holiday, or reminiscing about the past. And now we're getting older, and we don't have as much future left as we used to have. Let's start living in the present.

It's not going to be easy because we're all so used to thinking three steps ahead, worrying about what's next and rushing to catch up with ourselves. Try a very simple exercise: next time you're running a little late on the way to some place you know well – anywhere will do – put a little mental camera on your shoulder and focus it on your thoughts. Where are they? I'll bet you're not thinking about the texture of the floor under your feet, or the people around you, or the noise of the traffic. No, your mind will be way in front of your body, imagining walking through the next door, or the one after that, composing an apology for lateness. It might even be somewhere entirely different (working out what to eat tomorrow or what to wear on Saturday).

Now try bringing your thoughts back to where you are. Focus. It won't slow you down, in fact it might even speed you up because now you're going to be more alert to what's around you and more able to avoid potential hazards. And even better, you might notice that the world around you is interesting.

Once you've realised that your thoughts are always racing ahead, you'll find yourself intrigued by the challenge of living in the moment and you'll practise the art. At first you'll have to do the 'camera on the shoulder' bit but after a while you'll find that, more and more, you're experiencing life at one hundred percent.

Of course, that's when you'll begin to realise that lots of your moments aren't exactly thrilling. Get into the habit of stopping every so often and asking yourself, 'Am I enjoying this? Is this feeling one I want to have when I'm retired?' Forget about whether the activity is important, or even necessary. Instead, concentrate on your emotional state and work out which activities are fun, which ones make you feel content, and which ones are dull and need to be avoided like the plague.

**Do you feel less than glorious when you look in the mirror these days? Try IDEA 8, *The cry of the beholder.***

*Try another idea...*

**'Live out of your imagination, not your history.'**
STEPHEN COVEY

*Defining idea...*

**'I like the dreams of the future better than the history of the past.'**
PATRICK HENRY

*Defining idea...*

How did
it go?

**Q   Living in the moment doesn't grab me at all. How can anything I do now be as exciting as climbing in the Himalayas?**

*A   Think about what made that experience so exciting. Was it perhaps because you had to give your total concentration to deal with the challenges you were facing? Your challenges now might be different, but you can still get a kick out of achieving them.*

**Q   I enjoy reminiscing and people like to listen to me. What's wrong with that?**

*A   Ask yourself 'Can they vote with their feet?' If they can, that's fine. Carry on. If, however, you're reminiscing to a captive audience, watch their body language. If they have that glazed look that says 'Let me out,' and their feet keep turning to the door, you'd better cut the story short.*

**Q   I'd like to write about my experiences, but I need some motivation to do this. Any ideas?**

*A   Be ambitious and aim for publication, or aim a little lower and write something for your local paper or community magazine – they're always looking for interesting contributions. Better still, find out whether there are any organisations that might welcome you as a speaker. If it goes down a storm you might even take it on tour!*

## 2

# Book the bungee jump

**There's a growing trend for pensioners to take up physically challenging sports. Well, why not? Let's see what gets your adrenalin pumping.**

Even an hour's session at the gym, or a jog around the duck pond in the park will give you a bit of a high, but if you really want to inject some excitement there's a lot more to be had.

You could well be in better physical shape than you were in your twenties, but even if you're creaking at the seams a little there's no reason why you can't decide to push the boundaries. One of the best ways of keeping young, having fun and feeling that life's worth living is to do something that gets those hormones racing around your body.

Now, what gives me a kick is probably very different from what gets you excited, so there's not much point in my sitting here telling you to climb up a waterfall if that's your idea of a boring day out, but I can give you some idea of how to find the activity that'll give you a buzz.

*Here's an idea for you...* **Too nervous for daredevil sports? Book a lesson in a controlled environment, with an instructor watching your every move, lots of first-class equipment, and a handy defibrillator just in case you panic. I'm not sure there's a tame version of a bungee jump, but what about learning to ski on a dry ski slope, or practising scuba diving in the local pool?**

Pardon me for starting on a down note, but I think it's best to rule out the things that really give you the willies. If you throw up at the mere thought of standing on a cliff top, there's not much point in booking yourself a climbing holiday – at least until you've had some therapy to deal with your fear of heights. Terrified of drowning? Forget about deep sea diving or white water rafting (but you might want to consider swimming lessons).

At the other extreme, there's no real excitement in going for things you know you love because you've done them before. If you've climbed three mountains, well, yes, you'll probably still get a thrill out of climbing your fourth, but it's probably not the same thrill you get from tackling something entirely new is it? If you own a yacht and have spent every holiday for the past ten years sailing the Med, you probably still get a lot of pleasure from it, but the adrenalin won't be anywhere near the level it was on that first trip.

Choose what suits you best, whether it's one of those stomach-emptying rides at the theme park, a drive around the ring road at rush hour, or a plunge into the waters of Oz. It's easy to find scary sports. You can probably list a dozen without giving it too much thought (and you can try checking the Dangerless Aerial Sports Club website if you're stuck) but how do you draw the balance between terror and ennui? What would give you a thrill without doing you any physical or psychological harm? Work down this quick checklist:

- Do you have any physical limitations? These may make some activities obvious no-no's.

**Scared to try? Read IDEA 13,** *The voice that whispers in your ear.*

*Try another idea...*

- Are there things that genuinely terrify you, to the extent that you can have a serious panic attack when you face them (e.g enclosed spaces, wide open spaces, or spiders)? If so, unless you're prepared to get some therapy first, any activity that includes these things can be crossed off straight away.

- Are there things you've always avoided because they make you uncomfortable (e.g. large dogs, snakes, heights)? Now here's a rich vein of possibilities. One way we get our kicks is by feeling we're not quite in

*'The policy of being too cautious is the greatest risk of all.'*
JAWAHARLAL NEHRU

*Defining idea...*

control, so if you can organise something for yourself that takes you into contact with the thing that gives you the shivers, you'll get a whopping thrill out of the experience.

Oh, by the way, it's important that I tell you this: get your doctor's OK before you seize this idea. Get yourself insured if necessary. Don't take risks if you're not prepared to take responsibility for them.

*'You may be disappointed if you fail, but you are doomed if you don't try.'*
BEVERLY SILLS, singer

*Defining idea...*

How did
it go?

**Q** **I'd love to do something exciting but I've been ill for a while and I'm not up to doing much yet. Where do I start?**

*A* *Obviously check with your doctor first, then choose something that's suitable for your level of fitness. After all, if you've been stuck at home with flu for a fortnight, just walking down the road can move those hormones.*

**Q** **I recently booked a serious climbing holiday but I've never climbed before and I was refused cover by my travel insurers, so I felt I had to abandon the idea in case I had an accident over there but I still want to go. Is there any way I can get insured? Do you think I'm being over-cautious?**

*A* *Goodness, what were you aiming to climb? K2? You obviously frightened the underwriters silly. If you were being a bit ambitious, try something a little less adventurous and you'll probably get cover. I gather lots of people travel without it, but I'm a confirmed wimp when it comes to insurance – there's no way I'd risk being stuck in hospital abroad with no insurance cover!*

**Q** **I'm a bit of speed junkie (yes, at my age). Where can I get my fix?**

*A* *How about taking a turn around a race track with an instructor ready to take over as you test your nerves to their limit? Perhaps you could get your nearest and dearest to buy you a track day for your next birthday/anniversary.*

# 3

# Retire to work

**Jobs for the over fifties? You're having a laugh aren't you? There are more opportunities than there used to be, and with a little know-how you can track down a job that will suit you.**

Hardly anyone I know wants to give up work. They mostly want to leave their jobs and lots of them want to take their pension, but they're reluctant to hang up the briefcase or the boots forever.

A nice safe option is to negotiate with your employer to stay on, possibly as a part-timer, seasonal worker or consultant. This is the thing to do if you genuinely love your job or if you're seriously scared there won't be any other jobs if you give up the one you've got. But I reckon there will be jobs for us. I reckon there's going to be a shocking labour shortage as all of us baby boomers retire, and with new age discrimination laws we've got a fighting chance of finding paid work. But only if we're willing to change. Bear with me – I'm going to get on my soap box for a couple of paragraphs.

*Here's an idea for you...* **If you're struggling to get a full-time job, what about going for a more flexible option? There's a lot of part-time and shift work available these days. Or how about seasonal jobs? (I quite fancy having a go at that neat machine that stuffs Christmas trees into net stockings!)**

What we have to get our heads around is the fact that *our* jobs won't be there. We're too expensive (because of all the annual pay rises we've accumulated); we're too stale – we can do our jobs with our eyes closed; we've got as far as we're going, so we've lost the hunger that our juniors display, and that makes us less innovative, less exciting to work with; and we're blocking the route to promotion for some of those juniors who deserve a boost.

Retirement isn't like a normal job change. When we go out to look for a job to supplement the pension we can't expect to get higher status and more money than we had in the old job. Instead we need to be open to change, willing to learn and keen to contribute some of our experience and wisdom to whatever organisation we're joining.

OK, I've stopped ranting now. But you get the picture. If you start your job hunt with an open mind, you'll find something. It may be entirely different from anything you've done before, but that's fine.

Kick off by being sure about what you want from your new job so that you can target your job search. Do you badly need to earn some money, do you want a new challenge, or do you just want to get out of the house and meet new people?

What can you offer? Spend time producing a 'flexi-CV' – a detailed record of just about everything you've ever done, your skills, your expertise. Make sure it's in a table format that you can chop around into a series of mini-CVs to suit each prospective employer. Never send anyone the full monty – if you send a 14-page epic you won't even get an interview – and try to keep each mini-CV down to about two pages max.

**If this isn't for you, and you're already heading for the beach, read IDEA 9, *From here to eternity*, before you decide which flight to book.**

*Try another idea...*

There is ageism out there, so use every method you can think of when you're looking for a job. One of the most effective methods is the old-fashioned network. As ever, it's not what you know, but who you know, so tell friends and colleagues you're in the market. Then there are a few specialist over-fifties recruitment agencies around, so send an appropriate version of your CV along to each of them. In the UK, the government is currently keen to help us oldies get back to work, so try your local Job Centre. And if the job you want is likely to be advertised, don't forget to check national and local newspapers and trade magazines.

*'We live in a wonderful world that is full of beauty, charm and adventure. There is no end to the adventures that we can have if only we seek them with our eyes open.'*
JAWAHARLAL NEHRU

*Defining idea...*

If you get an interview remember the rules. They're just as important for pensioners as they are to young people. Dress appropriately, turn up on time – all the usual stuff – and, more importantly, do a bit of research on the employer, so they'll see you're genuinely interested in what you can do for them.

*'It is better to wear out than to rust out.'*
RICHARD CUMBERLAND, philosopher

*Defining idea...*

How did it go?

**Q   I've sent out loads of CVs but haven't had a single interview. Should I leave my age off?**

A   *Whatever your age, sending out your CV to local businesses tends to be the least successful way of getting a new job so it probably wouldn't increase your chances much if you deleted the age details. Give it a try but you should also try some of the other ways of finding work.*

**Q   I've had two interviews but no job offer. I feel really cross because I reckon I was perfect for both. Can I take action against them for age discrimination?**

A   *I doubt it, unless you've got some stunningly good evidence. I suggest you do a bit of a reality check before you consider taking action. Did you turn up on time? Did you wear the right clothes? How well did you answer their questions and perform on the psychological tests? How much do you know about the person who got the job?*

**Q   I've been offered a short-term contract. Should I think about taking it?**

A   *Short-term contracts often get rolled over, so you could end up with virtually a full-time job.*

# 4

# Just get out from under my feet, will you?

**Togetherness may be great for a weekend or a holiday, but it's not always so great when you and your partner are forced to share the same space full time. Anticipate problems and work out how to avoid them.**

Whether one or both of you has been working, there's going to be a huge adjustment when the two of you are at home.

It's probably slightly easier if you both intend to retire at the same time, but if your partner's been at home for more than a few months you might be about to stray into a minefield. I reckon there are three red flag areas: chores, hobbies and social lives.

If there's any possibility of a power struggle over who's going to do what chores around the house, deal with this one first. There are people who haven't spoken to each other for years because they couldn't agree how often the floor should be vacuumed. (And, at the other extreme, I know wives who are being driven quietly

Here's an idea for you...

**Identify a personal space and time for each of you. 'Space' doesn't mean a shelf in a cupboard – it means your own retreat where you can do your own thing.**

insane because their suddenly unoccupied husbands follow them around the house like devoted poodles.)

It's smart to work on the basis that whoever spots a job that needs doing is the person who gets on and does it, but if this sounds like a recipe for disaster in your household, go back to schooldays and draw up a rota to decide who does what, when and how often. Just to be fair, decide which jobs you both loathe and swap them around regularly.

Now: hobbies. If you don't have any, you need to get some or, as I hinted a minute ago, you'll drive your other half up the wall. Conversely, if you've been itching to get into your model railway as soon as you've escaped the day job (apparently men aged 40–50 are major buyers!) you could be storing up a heap of trouble.

If you don't think you have any hobbies, I should just mention that my definition of the word is pretty loose – it doesn't just mean collecting stamps and knitting. It includes things like playing sport, selling on eBay and researching your family tree. They're all examples of activities that take you away, physically or mentally, from your partner, and unless you've both agreed on what's reasonable, and what's intolerable, any one of them can be the cause of major stress. Your idea of 'a quick round of golf' may be your partner's idea of 'yet another afternoon spent on my own'; your insistence on explaining the details of your family tree to every new acquaintance may be your partner's personal hell of embarrassment. So, decide together what's reasonable behaviour when it comes to hobbies. Practice the art of compromise and be prepared to flex the agreement as time passes.

Then there's the social life. Not so difficult if you're both retiring together, because you can work it out as you grow into the new life. But it could be a bit of an issue if your partner's been at home for a while and has a flourishing network of friends. What are you going to do? Join her at the sewing circle and form a men's chapter?

**There's more than one thing that can cause partnership strife. Have a look at IDEA 6, *Use it or lose it.***

*Try another idea...*

I'm afraid there isn't really much option here: you have to talk to each other *a lot*. It's going to require tact, patience, kindness and the ability to compromise, and at the end each of you has to know that you have the freedom to see your own friends at least some of the time.

**'Don't compromise yourself. You are all you've got.'**
JANIS JOPLIN

*Defining idea...*

If you find you can sort out the chores but it's difficult to balance the hobbies or the social life, agree that you'll come to a short-term compromise, and that you'll review the whole arrangement in a month to see how it's working for each of you. That way you'll take some of the pressure off and give yourselves time to adjust.

**'Compromise. An amiable arrangement between husband and wife whereby they agree to let her have her own way.'**
Anon.

*Defining idea...*

How did
it go?

**Q**  **We've tried to compromise over her endless tennis games but things have just gone from bad to worse. On the odd occasion we're both at home we sit in separate rooms, and we hardly ever talk to each other now. Is it over?**

**A**  *I always remember someone telling me that a relationship is over when the basic courtesies are gone - little things like asking how someone's day has been, or passing the salt. Try reintroducing some of those and if things don't improve perhaps you could suggest a session with a marriage guidance counsellor?*

**Q**  **I'm retiring but my wife isn't. We've always shared the chores, but I get the distinct feeling that she's expecting me to do everything once I'm at home. I don't mind doing my bit, but do you agree it's unreasonable of her to expect a servant?**

**A**  *One man's reasonable is another's totalitarian state. Frankly, the only way to deal with this is to face it squarely. Talk to her about it and reach a compromise.*

**Q**  **Our house is tiny. Where are we both going to find our own 'space'?**

**A**  *You may need to get a bit creative - take turns using the spare room, or move the furniture around in the living room to free up a small corner. Then work out how much time you actually have available for hobbies and friends: 24 hours minus sleep, personal grooming, cooking and eating, household chores, etc. Divide your available time into two (not necessarily equal) sections: one section is for being together; the other is for time apart.*

# 5

# Spend it like Beckham?

**If you've always spent your income (or even more than your income) and you can't imagine how you'll cope on your pension, this one's for you. It's all about managing the budget.**

I once knew someone who was obviously worried about whether he'd cope on his pension, so one day I asked him whether he'd worked out a budget.

He amazed me by saying that, no, he was putting off doing that because it was going to be so time-consuming to go through everything he'd spent over the past year or so.

I'm not sure I ever convinced him that he'd got it upside down, but if you're a big spender I hope I can convince you that what you spend now is, to a large extent, irrelevant. All that matters is what you will be spending in future, and you're going to have to go back to the days of your penurious youth and remember the basic facts about budgeting. It's simple – if a bit tedious – to work out.

*Here's an idea for you...*

**Try living on your pension now, before you actually have to. Work out exactly what income you'll have (not forgetting that pensions are taxable). For the next six months, do your utmost to live on what you'll be getting.**

Find yourself a large pad of paper, a pen and a calculator. Get out your bills, credit card statements, bank statements and receipts for the last year and work through them, identifying every payment that will still need to be made when you retire. Include only the necessities of life – things like utilities, taxes, car maintenance, food. Total 'em up and see how much you've got left from your expected pension income so you can see how much you can afford to set aside for unexpected expenses (the lawn mower packs up), holidays, gifts and clothes.

If it's looking a bit tight, work back through your bills to see where you might be able to save some money. For example, it's usually cheaper to pay utilities by direct debit, and if you shop around you can save money on insurance premiums (never automatically accept a renewal quote – always check the rivals because you're almost bound to find a better deal).

As a priority, sort out any debts and if possible aim to clear them all before you retire. If you've got a wallet full of credit cards, cut most of them up and just stick to the ones that charge the least interest or, even better, use debit or charge cards from now on. Pay off the bills on the cards that charge the highest interest as fast as you can, and don't even consider consolidating all your debts unless you're one hundred percent sure you understand what it's going to cost you.

If you can afford it, stock up on basic household items in advance of your retirement. Instead of having another expensive restaurant meal, have a trip to town and use the cash you'd have spent on posh nosh to buy yourself a set of towels or some bed linen, or a spare iron. If you do this, you'll give yourself a breathing space when you retire, so you can get used to living on the reduced income without having to worry about affording the small but expensive necessities of life as they wear out.

Not sure what your pension will be? Read IDEA 18, *Where's the Enigma machine when you need it?*

Try another idea...

No matter how prepared you are, your domestic appliances (the ones that are really essential but really boring to buy, like washing machines, kettles and vacuum cleaners) will break down in the month after their guarantees expire. And have you noticed how these things always seem to work together to make life hell? There appears to be some kind of law that if the iron blows up on Tuesday the washing machine will seize up (full of water, naturally) on Wednesday. This means you will definitely need some savings. Start getting canny about spending now, so you can have a bit of spare cash ready. Save by never paying full price – buy at sale time, check out eBay, car boot sales, charity shops, markets.

'*Never spend your money before you have it.*'
THOMAS JEFFERSON

Defining idea...

'*Debt is the worst poverty.*'
THOMAS FULLER

Defining idea...

*How did it go?*

**Q**  **For the last six months I've tried to live on my pension income and it's obvious I'm not going to cope when I retire next year. I'm beginning to panic. Where do I go next?**

**A**  *Basically you've only got two options. You can re-examine your spending to see whether you can cut back on some of what you thought was essential, or you can get some extra income, either by retiring later or by taking a post-retirement job.*

**Q**  **None of this works for me because I'm so deep in debt. I keep hoping for a miracle – is there one?**

**A**  *If you're approaching retirement and you're insolvent you can no longer pretend that things will sort themselves out. Sit down, if necessary with an insolvency expert, and work out exactly how much you owe. You have various options, which range from informal arrangements with your creditors to the more serious formality of bankruptcy. No matter how dreadful these sound, any of them is better than living with the constant threat that someone will take you to court.*

**Q**  **I'm not really financially house-trained. How can I really practise living on my pension now?**

**A**  *To make it simple, use a current account as your pension-level account, and a deposit account as your 'untouchable' account. If, for example, you expect a pension income of 100 per week and you currently earn 500 per week, every payday you need to transfer 400 into the untouchable account, leaving the remaining 100 in the pension-level account.*

# 6

# Use it or lose it

**What's all that down there made of? Muscle! What does muscle do if it isn't used? It withers. You're never too old for sex, so get flexing.**

I've tried to locate a book that's specifically geared to the idea of pensioners having a great sex life, but all I've managed to find is the occasional coy reference to sexual dysfunction in the elderly and a couple of websites about impotence.

Now, I have to be fair. You could argue this means that sex life continues unchanged over the decades, and that books called *1000 Ways to an Orgasm* are aimed at all ages. But, forgive the cynicism, I reckon it's because people who write sex books assume that people over sixty (some men, and all pop stars excepted) don't have sex any more. Far too disgusting to contemplate, isn't it? All those wrinkles and dangling folds of skin? Yeuk.

Let me say it, loudly and clearly. People over sixty have sex. People of all ages (yes, women, too) have sex.

Here's an idea for you... **If everything's working as it should but the thing you're struggling to raise is your enthusiasm, maybe you and your partner are just a bit bored with the same old routine. If so, just as sex isn't the prerogative of the young, neither are sex aids forbidden to wrinklies. It could be just what you need to add some spice to your life.**

There. I feel better now.

So, I hear you ask, why do we need a sex book if we can read the same ones everyone else reads? Regretfully, I have to admit that not everyone over sixty finds it easy to enjoy their sex life in the way they used to. It's not just that muscles need regular use to keep them in shape – there are other, more sinister problems to deal with and these are the ones no one seems to want to talk about out loud.

## MEN

Mother Nature knows how to hit where it hurts doesn't she? Impotence is men's deepest horror and their greatest secret. Let's bring it out of the closet (if you see what I mean). It's nothing to be ashamed about. Hey, if you can cope with the embarrassment of open-plan changing rooms, what's so difficult about admitting to a common problem?

And it is common. Apparently as many as one in ten men have difficulty with their erections – and that ratio increases with age. If you've had the problem for more than a couple of months there could be various physical causes, such as coronary heart disease or diabetes. The side effects of some drugs can also be the cause of the problem, and lifestyle can be a factor too (e.g. smoking, drugs, poor diet, too much alcohol); and, of course, there are psychological reasons for impotence.

The first stop is your doctor. Don't waste time. I don't want to be rude, but I think you're insane if you don't get it sorted just because you're too embarrassed to tell the doctor. Either there'll be a physical cause that can be treated, or he can refer you to a specialist clinic, or he can recommend therapy. Go on – put a big grin on your face and promise yourself that you're going to do everything you can to have a great sex life again!

**If you want great sex you need to be fit and healthy. Read IDEA 19, *VO2 Max it*, and revitalise all the bits.**

*Try another idea…*

## WOMEN

We don't have the pressure to perform that men have to deal with, but there are still factors that can ruin our sex life as we get older. Post-menopausal women can suffer from (take a deep breath) atrophic vaginitis. Sounds appalling doesn't it? Basically it means what I said at the top of the chapter – the muscles lose their elasticity, with the added complication that the vagina becomes dry. Don't panic – it's treatable, with a range of things that include oestrogen cream (from the doctor), a spoonful of oil a day (apparently that lubricates everything, something I don't really want to think about too much) and water-soluble lubricants (from the local pharmacist). You also need to exercise, and you should include general exercises plus some that are specifically targeted, such as Kegel exercises, which your doctor will explain to you.

*'Caresses, expressions of one sort or another, are necessary to the life of the affections as leaves are to the life of a tree. If they are wholly restrained, love will die at the roots.'*
NATHANIEL HAWTHORNE

*Defining idea…*

*'The more we do, the more we can do.'*
WILLIAM HAZLITT

*Defining idea…*

How did
it go?

**Q**  **I lost interest in sex a while ago, and though it worries me that I don't ever seem to get aroused I feel I can't possibly go to my doctor – I'd be far too embarrassed at my age. How can I summon up the courage to make that trip to the surgery.**

**A**  *It's all about perspective. When you're a kid you think it's gross when you realise that people in their forties (or even thirties) have sex, but your doctor knows better. He'll understand and he'll give you factual advice and practical help.*

**Q**  **My doctor's sorted out the physical problems but my partner and I are really struggling to get started again after such a long time. How do we begin?**

**A**  *Why not start with gentle caresses and a firm policy of 'sex is not allowed unless we can't restrain ourselves any longer'? The more you explore each others' bodies the more anxious you'll be to get going!*

**Q**  **We'd like to experiment with some sex aids. Where can we buy these?**

**A**  *Get yourself down to the high street. If you've never bought an erotic book or video, or a sex toy before, take heart – they've moved from being the province of seedy shops and now they're big business. You might even, one day soon, find some on the shelves of your local chemist. And don't forget the internet, though be warned that searches for anything of this nature may give you more than you bargained for!*

# 7
# Don't act your age

**Hey. This is going to be great. It'll be the first time since you were a child that you'll have the chance to have fun without feeling guilty. Can you even remember what fun is? Remind yourself of the things that make you laugh.**

For most of us, the trouble with being a grown-up is that we've got ourselves trapped in the treadmill of responsibility and we've kept fun firmly in its place for years.

If, like me, you have offspring you'll have had some fun when your kids were small (and that was pretty well balanced, what with the nappies and the chauffeuring duties). If we're lucky we've had the odd weekend away, an occasional night out, an annual holiday, even the dreaded office Christmas party. But these things have often been squished into a hectic diary and we've turned up grouchy, begrudging the time and effort we've had to make, when we could have been at home zonked out in front of the telly. We don't, generally, get real fun, and it's so sad that we think that's how it should be.

Here's an idea for you...

**Today, and every day from now one, set aside a small period of time – anything from ten minutes to an hour – and do something you enjoy. It could be serious fun (roller-blading down the High Street?) or it could be something really small. It doesn't matter what it is – go window shopping; cuddle the cat; kick leaves – just try for something different every day and, when you do it, do it one hundred percent.**

I know this is true for me, because when I see a grown-up having real fun I think to myself 'Stupid idiot. He needs to grow up.' And, yes, I know that sounds like blatant sexism, but it usually is a man. For years I've made jokes about some men not growing up, and now I find the joke's on me. They've got it right all along.

What's the secret to fun? I can hardly remember. What were the real fun times? For me, climbing Dunns River Falls was fun; getting lost in the music at rock concerts was fun; punting on the Cam on a hot summer's day was fun; trying to play tennis last year (after a forty-year break) was fun, if a trifle embarrassing.

What were the fun times for you? When you've remembered them, ask yourself what was it that made them fun? How did you feel? The common denominator for me is that these things were all different from the things I normally do – and sometimes even a bit scary. (Cynics amongst you, stop laughing. Punting on the Cam is a seriously dangerous activity unless, like me, you're lucky enough to have an expert handling the pole rather than some idiot undergraduate who wants to show off.)

Defining idea...

**'Age does not depend upon years, but upon temperament and health. Some men are born old, and some never grow so.'**
TRYON EDWARDS, American theologian

Your idea of fun is bound to be quite different from mine. You may have had fun trudging through the mud and facing the portaloos at pop festivals; you might get your thrills from racing round a Caribbean bay on an old tyre, pulled by a motor boat (I'm told it's like high-speed colonic irrigation). Train spotting or chess might be the activities that got your adrenalin going over the years. But the common denominator must, surely, be laughter? (Which, equally surely, must rule out train spotting?) If we're not laughing – or at least smiling – we're not really having fun are we? Nor are we experiencing the massive physiological benefits of laughter, which floods our bodies with happy hormones, relieves stress and is a thoroughly healthy activity.

**IDEA 27, *A brand named 'old',* will put the icing on the cake of your new life.**

*Try another idea...*

Now, how do we recapture that feeling without necessarily having to repeat the experience? Since my kicks come from trying something new, my plan is to find some activities that are different – things I'd never even thought of doing before. Hmm, learn to tango perhaps? What does it for you? Whatever it is, commit to it by building it into your life so you have lots to look forward to over the next few months. Booking lessons, arranging dates with friends and paying in advance are all good ways of making sure you won't chicken out in favour of the sofa.

*'Although an old man, I am but a young gardener.'*
THOMAS JEFFERSON

*Defining idea...*

*'I refuse to admit I'm more than fifty-two, even if that does make my sons illegitimate.'*
LADY ASTOR

*Defining idea...*

27

*How did it go?*

**Q** **Fun for me used to be snowboarding, and I've spent many holidays on the slopes, but last time I tried it was too much like hard work and I ended up aching from head to foot. There's nothing else that has quite that kick for me. Are my days of real fun gone?**

*A* *Not at all. Life changes, and we face new challenges. If you were bedridden you'd probably get a kick out of making it to the bathroom on your own (perhaps not quite 'fun' though). Find something new. But whatever you choose to do, concentrate entirely on your chosen activity, and for a few minutes' play you'll get a day's worth of that heady feeling that tells you life's worth living.*

**Q** **My idea of fun is to go dancing but my husband can't dance and refuses point blank to join me, though he doesn't mind if I go out on my own. Any ideas how I can convince him that dancing's not threatening?**

*A* *What about striking a bargain? What does he enjoy that you don't? Go along with him and give it a try, if he agrees to have dance lessons with you.*

# 8

# The cry of the beholder

**We've all heard the bitchy comments: 'Do you think he's wearing a toupee?' 'Look at her! Has she had another face lift?' Ignore the critics. Look good and be proud of yourself.**

It drives me crazy. I buy the magazine because its cover promises me it'll help me update my make-up to suit my age.

I eagerly turn the pages, past the inevitable teens and twenties, to the poor thirty-year olds (when wrinkles are getting really bad). Wow! There's a page for forty-year olds. Here goes, let's see what's on the next page: 'Win a winter holiday in St Lucia.' Yet again, I don't exist!

Of course, this whinge is from a woman's point of view. If you're a man in your fifties and you fancy a bit of cosmetic enhancement you might as well give up now because it's much worse for you. The average man has no chance of finding magazine guidance unless he's a twenty-year-old stud with a six-pack and oiled skin.

Here's an idea for you... **It's really easy to get a makeover whatever age you are. Walk into any store and hint to one of the over-made-up girls in pristine white coats that you've got some serious money to spend on the right make-up. You'll be sitting there with a towel round your shoulders before you can catch your breath. Try the same trick in three or four stores with different products, then pick the best from each for your new look.**

To be fair, I've seen a few more articles recently that are aimed at women in their fifties, but that's only because the baby boomers are reaching that stage of decrepitude and they've got money to spend. But there's nothing much out there for pensioners, possibly because the manufacturers haven't yet realised there's a market or (more likely) because the average editor can't believe anyone over sixty has any chance of looking nice.

Most of us women tend to stick to the same old beauty regime we've been using for years or, just as bad, give up wearing make-up entirely because it's too much trouble or because no one looks at us anyway. If you're seeking a new look to go with your newly retired status, it's important to include your beauty regime in the makeover.

## MAKE-UP FOR PENSIONERS

From the little that's out there I've worked out the following rules.

Foundation should be tested on your face (not on your hands, which are an entirely different colour), and if you're wrinkled go for something light and liquid so it doesn't settle into the grooves. Eye shadow should be more muted than you wore in your twenties and thirties, but you can go for a good lash-thickening mascara. Outline your lips with a lip pencil to stop your lipstick bleeding and avoid strong colours (which tend to make old women look a bit like Bette Davies in *What Ever Happened to Baby Jane?*). Finally, don't keep make-up for too long, because it harbours bacteria – not nice.

If you've checked out the mags for ideas for over-fifties and are now thoroughly irritated, have a look at IDEA 14, *The march of age.*

*Try another idea...*

By the way, not all products suit all people, so if you feel like splashing out why not find a professional make-up artist? You'll find them advertising in magazines and on the internet and they will (at no small cost I'm afraid) give you a couple of hours of their time in order to find the right products and show you how to apply them.

## FACE SHAPING FOR PENSIONERS

This is probably the time when all those green-tinted concealers start to come into their own. And it's not just green (which tones down the red areas). There are highlighters for, well, highlighting the best bits. There are pink and orange tints for concealing the dark bits. In fact you can buy tinted foundation that'll cover just about anything. If you decide to have a go, use them sparingly and make sure you blend them in well so there's no harsh line of colour across your face or neck.

'Half the work that is done in this world is to make things appear what they are not.'
ELIAS ROOT BEADLE, American clergyman

*Defining idea...*

31

## COSMETIC SURGERY

Wouldn't do it myself (pain-averse), but I can't see why people are so bitchy about people who do. If you've wanted a nose job all your life, no, it's not too late to get it done. If you're desperately unhappy about the wrinkles and think a face lift's the answer, as long as you can answer a couple of basic questions, why not go for it? The questions?

- Have you checked the risks? There are risks to any surgery, particularly as you get older, and there are specific risks to each type of surgery (you've seen the horror programmes – odd-sized boobs, over-stretched faces).

- Will it make you feel better? Sometimes the problem's internal rather than external, so be sure you don't just have a distorted body image. See a therapist if necessary before you go for the treatment.

**Q** **I've tried half a dozen different ranges of eye make-up but they all irritate me – even the hypo-allergenic ranges. Is there a good alternative?**

*How did it go?*

**A** *Have you changed your make-up brushes lately? They harbour bacteria too, and it might just be that they're causing the problem.*

**Q** **I'm thinking of going abroad for liposuction. Will it be safe?**

**A** *Wherever you go for cosmetic surgery you need to be sure that your surgeon is properly qualified and registered. Check with the country's regulatory body that he or she is on their list and find out whether there are any specialist qualifications you should be looking for.*

**Q** **I'm not sure if I should still wear make-up: the geriatric hooker look just isn't me! What am I doing wrong?**

**A** *Badly applied make-up always looks dreadful, but it's harder to get it right when you get older because skin tone deteriorates and skin colour changes. It's unlikely the youth-obsessed magazines will help, so maybe you should think about getting advice from a professional make-up artist. They really can make a difference.*

33

# 9

# From here to eternity

**Some people think retirement's just one long holiday. But exactly what is a holiday for you? What makes it different from daily life? Have another look at your holiday plans before you settle for the usual comfort zone.**

You may be lucky. You may love getting away from it all, have plenty of cash stashed away to travel all the time during your retirement, and be already packed and ready for the taxi to the airport on day one of your retirement.

Most of us, however, aren't going to have the finance available to do that – we'll be spending the majority of our time in our own homes.

In fact, I once knew a couple who spent most of their retirement either planning their next trip abroad or talking incessantly about previous trips. It always seemed to me that they'd got the balance wrong, because it was obvious that their home

Here's an idea for you... **Did you know you can swap your home with someone from another country for a few weeks? House-swap companies can arrange this for you, or maybe you already know someone living overseas who'd love the chance to come back and see old friends from the comfort of your home, while you enjoy theirs?**

life and, to be honest, their home itself, gave them no pleasure – so they escaped into a fantasy-land of holiday dreams. For years I longed to say, 'Why don't you spend some of this money on doing up your house?' but I never found the courage. And then it was too late: serious illness entered their lives, and they were stuck in their uncomfortable home with all dreams ended. That's why I've included so much in this book about living life to the full at home, but it doesn't mean you can't have some truly great holidays too.

Obviously your choice of getaways is, to a large extent, dependent on how much you can spend, but even a limited budget and a chicken-heart doesn't mean you can't be a little adventurous. Walking (or lurching if you prefer) from Guinness to Guinness in the Irish Republic, or even meandering along the Thames path from one themed pub to the next, doesn't cost the earth and is very unthreatening if you've never tried it before.

If you've spent every holiday on the beach at Marbella, or in a caravan in Whitby, or even climbing in the Andes, and you're not quite sure what kind of alternative holiday might appeal to you, how about trying a taster session to see whether you're missing some real fun? As a dry-run for a full spa holiday, book in for a full day at a local health farm; if you've thought about pony trekking in Lesotho, get yourself a course of riding lessons to see how you cope with the saddle sores. In half an hour on the internet I managed to find taster sessions for most adventure holidays within a hundred miles of my home – though I'll admit I failed miserably in my efforts to find something in the UK that even remotely resembled an African safari.

Prefer a panorama? Good Lord, where do you start? No matter how many years are left, life's always going to be just too short to see everything isn't it? Over the next month write down everywhere you've ever dreamt of seeing – the famous buildings, the art, the scenery, the people. Which are the ones you must see? Can you combine or do you need separate trips? Don't hang around – if you don't act on your dreams they'll never come true. As soon as your list's complete, pick up an armful of holiday brochures and get stuck in.

And if none of this works for you, there's more! If you can't face another city tour or beach holiday, how about a learning holiday? I've found: cooking, language, painting, canoeing, history, dancing…too many to list.

**If you hate being retired and you're looking for an escape rather than a holiday, think again. Read IDEA 40, *I used to be someone, but now I'm retired*, and learn to enjoy your new status.**

*Try another idea…*

*'And I'd like to roll to Rio Some day before I'm Old!'*
RUDYARD KIPLING

*Defining idea…*

*'I dislike feeling at home when I'm abroad.'*
GEORGE BERNARD SHAW

*Defining idea…*

**How did it go?**

**Q** **I'd love to try new places but I bought a really expensive timeshare apartment in Spain and I feel I have to go out there for three weeks a year just to get my money's worth. I regret buying the place now, but how can I sell it?**

**A** *Not good news, I'm afraid. I'm told that the resale price of a timeshare can be as low as 30% of the original cost and even at its best you're likely to make a hefty loss. To sell it you'll need to find an agent who's prepared to act for you. As an alternative, have you thought about finding other people in the same situation and doing an annual swap?*

**Q** **Last time we tried holidaying with friends we ended up not speaking to them again. Do you think it ever works?**

**A** *Yes, it can work – I've proved it in the past. The trick is to be very courteous. If someone in the party wants to lie on the beach while you want to climb a mountain, there's no reason why she should have to give up her ideal day to make your holiday better. Separate, give each other plenty of space, and meet up in the evenings at the local bar.*

**Q** **I've thought about doing a house swap as a cheap holiday. How do I avoid the pitfalls?**

**A** *The easiest way is to use a professional house-swap company. Swapping with old and trusted friends is the next best option (check that your household insurance covers the period you're away). If you go solo and arrange your own swap with strangers, make sure you take proper safeguards: references at the very least, and perhaps a deposit to cover damage.*

# 10

# Where there's a way... there's a will

**It can be a weight off your mind to know you've found a way to take care of your loved ones after you pop your clogs. Make sure now that they can manage after you're gone.**

*Only death and taxes are certain — and they go hand in hand. If you don't plan for your death the taxman wins.*

The best thing you can do is to make your financial arrangements as clear as possible and take some of the load off your loved ones when they need it most.

## MAKE A WILL

It's amazing how many people put this off as if, somehow, the very act of making a will is going to make it more likely that they'll die. *Newsflash:* it's going to happen whether you've left your estate in order or not!

If you haven't written your will already, or if you haven't revised it since your children were babies (or since before you won the lottery), this is priority number

*Here's an idea for you...* **Think about organising your own funeral. It sounds a bit morbid, but you can take a lot of the stress off your loved ones this way. You can pay for it, choose your own coffin, order flowers, decide on the kind of service you want and even shock everyone with your funky choice of music.**

one. Not making a will equals major hassles for your family. Your property won't go where you expect it to go (intestacy rules are spectacularly illogical) and it'll take forever to go anywhere at all.

You can get a proforma will form to fill in yourself in most good stationers. I have to admit I have a personal objection to them because the language of wills is precise and it's easy to make mistakes if you have a DIY job. Still, if you don't own much and you don't have zillions of people to leave it to (and you're absolutely clear about who will get what) you may want to go for this option. If you do decide to go it alone, keep your language very clear and simple so you don't end up leaving everything to the cat because some common word you've used has a different meaning in law.

*Defining idea...* **'Let us not be content to wait and see what will happen, but give us the determination to make the right things happen.'**
PETER MARSHALL, psychologist

If you have more than a bit of cash to leave, a solicitor will give you advice on how best to arrange your bequests so that you minimise tax liabilities. If you're concerned about the cost involved (and you needn't be, because it's pretty cheap) just picture the lawyers rubbing their hands with glee at the prospect of their fees for sorting out the mess you've left. You can also give money away (every country has different limits) but don't hang around because you need to live for a number of years after the gift or it'll be hammered for tax when you die.

**If you're the one who's been left to grieve, learn how to relax with IDEA 15, *Don't do it*.**

*Try another idea...*

## SORT YOUR PAPERS

The person who's going to be dealing with your possessions after you've gone will need to have them in some kind of order that makes sense. If you keep bills and receipts, old letters, recipes and gardening tips in a cardboard box under the cobwebs in the shed, you're making sure that some poor sap will have to spend a gruesome afternoon turning over papers, one at a time, to make sure they're not missing a book full of rare stamps or a treasure map. You don't have to spend a fortune – even one of those concertina A–Z files is better than a messy pile of papers.

## MAKE FINANCIAL PROVISIONS

It's bad enough dealing with the death of someone you love, without lying awake at night worrying about whether you've got enough money to get you through the next month. If you have dependents, take out life assurance, even if it's only for a small sum that'll be enough to tide them over for a short while. Don't forget to tell them you've done it, so they'll know they are provided for.

*'I do not believe in a fate that falls on men however they act; but I do believe in a fate that falls on them unless they act.'*
G. K. CHESTERTON

*Defining idea...*

41

**How did it go?**

**Q** **I'm alone in the world so I've already organised my funeral. Now I'd like to make a will, but I've got nobody to leave my money to. I always think it's really sad when people leave everything to charity. Any ideas?**

**A** *A lot of charities depend on people's bequests so there's no reason why you shouldn't feel proud to help. But, if you'd like to have a person at the end of your bequest, what about sponsoring a child, or becoming a charitable friend to a school in a Third World country? You can send donations and write letters and, when you die, your money will go to people you've grown to know.*

**Q** **My partner's hopeless with money – I look after everything. I just know he'll get himself in a financial mess if I die first. Is there anything else I can do to help him?**

**A** *If you deal with everything I guess he might well get in a mess, because it's very difficult to make sense of someone else's financial records. He's probably thought of this himself and might welcome becoming more involved so that he understands what's what – and where everything's kept.*

**Q** **I can't bear funerals where everyone stands around looking miserable. How can I go out with a bang?**

**A** *Organise your own wake: that'll make sure they'll remember you! You get a neat little envelope to hand over to your next of kin so all they have to do is make a phone call to set the whole thing in motion.*

# 11

# Safety first?

**Are pensioners more vulnerable to crime than other people? Well, no, but if you're worried, do something to help yourself anyway.**

There's an undying perception that old people are more at risk of violent crime than anyone else in our community, but the statistics just don't support that view.

Still, it's sensible to take some basic precautions to make yourself feel more confident, and there are three basic steps you might consider.

1. *Burglars go for easy targets.* Make sure you've got good door and window locks. If you're really nervous and can afford it, double-glaze your windows and doors for extra security.

2. *Fit an alarm.* They're not cheap (and they're a pain in the neck when they go wrong) but burglars might just avoid your house if they see one. You'll get a reduction on your insurance premium, too.

Here's an idea for you... **Have some fun and get some confidence by taking self-defence classes. Lots of organisations run them and, if you're female and nervous about going to a mixed class, some of them are run for women only.**

3.  *Use your common sense.* Lock windows and doors. Don't let strangers in the house. Keep your keys safe – and that doesn't mean: under the front door mat; on a piece of string tied through the letterbox (really, you should know better); on a table or hook just beside the door (because burglars put hooks through the letter box to fish 'em out).

Now, what about outside the home? The best way to protect yourself is to avoid being in dangerous situations. Walking down dark alleys or travelling home on near-empty trains late at night is just asking for trouble. Much better to leave early, travel with a friend, or take a licensed taxicab.

If you can't avoid a lone journey you need to look confident and in control – don't, whatever you do, crawl along looking like a victim; don't show off the Rolex or your fancy new phone. If you become really scared, you need to *act*. I can't tell you how many times I've been walking home from the station in the dark and I've become aware of someone following me. What do I do? Do I look around and make sure it's some other poor sap on the way home from work? Or do I run home as fast as I can? Neither. I'm too embarrassed to run and too scared to look round and check whether the follower looks suspicious. To hell with looking a fool. Turn around and see who it is.

Defining idea... **'We live in an age when pizza gets to your home before the police.'**
JEFF MARDER, American comedian

If you don't like the look of them, run. Scream if you want. Go and knock on someone's door and tell them you're being followed.

Sometimes there's nowhere to run, and no one to help. If you can't ignore or defuse the situation, try this technique, which worked for me recently when two young men were behaving very badly on an empty train and scaring me silly. When one of them started harassing me I asked him, 'How old are you? About twelve? Because that's how you're acting.' I've never seen anything more effective. He and his pal kinda shrunk into the seat and slunk off at the next station, looking total prats.

I hear the critics. What if that hadn't worked? Well, I wouldn't have been any worse off would I? I should, of course, have been sitting nearer to the alarm in the first place. But I do carry a mobile phone and I would have got off at the next station. Perhaps I might add a whistle, or a personal alarm?

**If you're nervous because you're on your own so much, why not read IDEA 23, *Only the lonely*?**

*Try another idea...*

*'When we were children, we used to think that when we were grown-up we would no longer be vulnerable. But to grow up is to accept vulnerability...To be alive is to be vulnerable.'*
MADELEINE L'ENGLE, American writer

*Defining idea...*

**How did it go?**

**Q** **The house next door was burgled last month, and I'm now very nervous. I don't feel so bad when I'm at home, but I'm away a lot, and even though I leave the lights on timers I'm always terrified about what I'll find when I get home. Is there anything else I can do?**

**A** *Lots of people put timers on their lights while they're away, so it looks as though there's someone in. I'm not sure this is very effective – anyone watching for a while can easily see there's no one in the house. Have you thought about getting a house sitter to pop in a couple of times a day just to draw curtains and check that everything's OK? If you can't afford to pay a professional (who, of course, would supply references) could you, perhaps, take a lodger so you don't have to leave the house entirely empty?*

**Q** **I have a garden thief. Someone's stealing my plants and, worse, I've lost three of my four garden gnomes. What can I do about this?**

**A** *You could have a motion-sensor light installed or, if that's too drastic for a few gnomes, why don't you paint their hats in that neat non-drying paint? You'll be able to spot your thief from the blue hands!*

**Q** **Where can I find out about self-defence classes?**

**A** *Have a word at the local police station or further education college or check out your local newspaper. Alternatively, do what I did when I found myself unexpectedly living alone. I joined a martial arts club. (I met my new husband there and spent more time falling in love than learning, but it was great fun.)*

# 12

# Chocolate is bad for you

**And so are cakes, biscuits, sweets...and diets. But obesity puts you in the risk zone for illness so don't ignore it. Bin the diet books and look at better ways of keeping your weight under control.**

Isn't it maddening how some people can eat as much as they want and stay slim, while others of us only have to walk past a cake to put on pounds?

The trouble is, the amount we eat isn't the only factor we have to think about because we all use up our calories at different rates. For example, my body works at top efficiency on the minimum fuel possible and kindly stores the rest as fat, while my husband radiates heat and burns up calories just by lying on the sofa reading the paper. You may be unfortunate enough to have to drive miles to the nearest bakery shop; or you may be lucky and live over one. You may go to the gym for an hour every night; or you may be a couch potato.

**Check your cholesterol levels, either with a home kit, or get your doctor to do this. And how about seeing if your blood pressure and sugar levels are OK? As you get older, it's worth keeping even closer tabs on these basic health markers. And it's never too late to get some good eating habits under your belt.**

What this tells us is that no two people can follow the same diet and achieve the same outcome. So I'm not suggesting that we need yet another new, faddy diet for our retirement years. What we need is an easy and nutritious eating plan for the rest of our lives. Here's mine – you don't need to weigh yourself, or your food, and there are only three rules:

- *Accept that calorie needs differ.* Your eating plan has to be different from mine, because your body doesn't use and store calories in the same way as mine, your exercise level isn't the same as mine, and your lifestyle is different from mine. It's unfair of course, but we all know that life's unfair, don't we?

- *Accept that portion size matters.* Over the last few years we've all been fooled into thinking that restaurant portions are 'normal'. They're not. Think back to your teens – did you ever go to restaurants that served 16oz steaks? (Texans please don't write in. I know you grew up in the land of the cow but some of us grew up with post-war austerity and didn't know what a restaurant was, never mind beef.)

- *Accept that this is a way of life.* In fact I've christened this the MUM eating plan (Moderate Until Monday). It lasts for a week and, just like all those diets you've tried, it starts every week on Monday. The trick in the tail is that this plan lasts for seven days, not just till Monday lunchtime!

Before you start, you need to work down this trail of questions.

1. Try on a favourite old outfit. How does it fit? Too tight? Too loose? Or about the same? Have you bought new clothes this season because last year's are too big, or too small?

2. Based on that test, over the past year have you put on weight, lost weight or stayed about the same? You don't need to weigh yourself unless you're really unhappy about guessing, because, deep down, you probably know roughly what the answer's going to be.

If you reckon you've lost weight but need to lose more, keep up what you're doing for another season, then go back to question 1.

If you've gained weight, or stayed about the same (and are sure you're still overweight), you're eating too much. Eat normally for a week, noting carefully the portion sizes you're getting through. Then adjust your portions, so you're eating the same amount of fruit and

*Try another idea...*

**Top off your new fit image with IDEA 21, *Don't split hairs.***

*Defining idea...*

'*The second day of a diet is always easier than the first. By the second day you're off it.*'
JACKIE GLEASON

49

*Defining idea...*

'**Researchers have discovered that chocolate produces some of the same reactions in the brain as marijuana. The researchers also discovered other similarities between the two, but can't remember what they are.**'
MATT LAUER, TV anchor

vegetables (unless they're deep-fried, which is cheating) but eating a little less of everything else. You can either put less on your plate or leave a bit of everything that's offered to you. Make sure you drink plenty of water.

Keep up the reduced portions for a month and try on the outfit again. If it's still tight, cut down a bit more; if it's looser you're on the right track. If it falls off you, well, you've been a bit too strict with yourself haven't you?

**Q** **I've been dieting for ages, and I've followed the MUM plan for a couple of months. I know my clothes are much looser, but no matter how much I cut down I can't seem to get to the shape I want. What am I doing wrong?**

*How did it go?*

**A** *You're ringing alarm bells here. This eating plan depends on total honesty, and if you've a seriously distorted body image it's not going to work for you – because you may never be convinced that you're thin enough. Can I suggest you go along to your doctor and check out whether you are really overweight before you continue?*

**Q** **You haven't mentioned alcohol. How much can I drink?**

**A** *Sad to say it's sensible to cut down on the booze in the same way that you cut down on the food. In any event you shouldn't be drinking more than the recommended limits.*

**Q** **Have you got a simple eating plan I can use?**

**A** *Follow this daily guide for a week to adjust your portion sizes and nutrient balance. Starchy foods like bread, rice or potato should fill at least a third of your plate. Eat five portions of fruit and vegetables. Have two to three portions of dairy foods. Portion sizes vary (obviously, you can have more skimmed milk than you can cream). A portion of cheese is about the size of a die. Have two tablespoons of oil, or four teaspoons of butter. Eat two or three portions of proteins (like fish, meat or nuts), each about the size of a pack of cards.*

# 13

# The voice that whispers in your ear

**You know what I mean. That insidious inner demon that tells you 'You're not good enough.' Well the demon's had a good run but now's the time to get rid of it forever and boost your self-image.**

Believe it or not you can change your mind about the things that scare you. It's never too late.

I couldn't swim, so the weekly swimming lesson was one of the many reasons my schooldays were horrible. A couple of years back I finally plucked up courage to have lessons and one day, while I was struggling in the baby pool, I overheard my teacher talking about me: 'Oh, she'll be fine once she's decided not to be scared.' I was so annoyed with myself that I was doing the backstroke within a fortnight.

We can all do this. If you want to spend the winter in Spain but are scared of flying, you can decide not to be scared. (Honestly.) If you'd love to paint but don't think you have any talent, decide you damned well have. The only barrier is anxiety and there's a technique for dealing with anxiety: just tell yourself 'It's only anxiety. If I work through it, I'll be less anxious next time.'

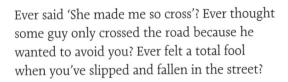

Here's an idea for you...

**Give your inner demon an identity. Work out where it's sitting and imagine what it looks like and what it sounds like; then name it. Be imaginative – personalise the blasted thing. Fix the look and sound of your demon in your mind, then grab hold of the creature and throw it as far away as you can. It'll find its way back sooner or later, but you may be surprised at how long it takes.**

Ever said 'She made me so cross'? Ever thought some guy only crossed the road because he wanted to avoid you? Ever felt a total fool when you've slipped and fallen in the street?

We all constantly 'talk' to ourselves even though we're not aware of it half the time. We rehearse what we're going to say before some difficult meeting; we imagine how situations are going to develop; we imagine what other people are thinking. Sometimes we're so busy listening to ourselves that we miss what everyone else is saying. Sometimes before a daunting task we're so wrapped up in the nerve-wrenching dialogue we're having with ourselves that we're defeated before we even begin.

Once you've realised that the demon is there, it's easier to defeat it. Here are two great techniques.

The best technique is to look forwards. Let's imagine you're nervous about walking into a room full of people. The demon will try to make you think about making a fool of

**Tackle one anxiety at a time with IDEA 29, *Eating the elephant.***

*Try another idea...*

yourself, looking stupid, saying something idiotic. Shove it away. Sit down quietly and think about being a success. Begin by remembering someone you respect – remember how they walk into a room, how they move, what they say. Then put yourself in their shoes. Visualise yourself walking into that room, moving confidently, making small talk. Repeat three times daily and gear yourself up for success.

The other technique is to master your demon by looking backwards. Think back to a recent situation where you felt upset but, for the moment, ignore how you felt and concentrate on the facts. What exactly happened? What did you say? What did others say? What did you do? How were you standing?

Next, start to remember how you felt. Concentrate hard on those emotions. Were you angry, scared, embarrassed? What were you saying to yourself? What have you said to yourself since? Write it all down.

*'You cannot run away from weakness; you must some time fight it out or perish; and if that be so why not now and where you stand?'*
ROBERT LOUIS STEVENSON

*Defining idea...*

55

Did your demon jump to conclusions? Recognise any of these?

- All or nothing thinking – nothing went right; it was a total disaster. (Oh, come on now, did your pants fall down too?)

- Ignoring the truth – I never do anything right. (Really? You bought this book didn't you?)

- Mind reading – she's thinking how fat I've got. (How do you know what she's thinking. Maybe she's listening to her inner demon, eh?)

- Prophesying – I just know the dentist is going to find something wrong. (Look at the facts. How often have you had a clean bill of health from him?)

- Judging – I should have got there sooner. She wouldn't have fallen. (Why? Are you perfect? Can you always predict what's going to happen? Is everything your responsibility?)

- Labelling – I'm a complete idiot. (No, you just made a mistake).

**Q** **I had to walk into a room full of strangers yesterday and, guess what? I forgot everything I'd worked on as soon as I opened the door. My face went brick red. Please, is there any way I can stop blushing?**

How did it go?

**A** *So, you blushed. Did the world end? Did everyone laugh at you? No. Most people probably didn't even notice; those who did probably made a mental note that you were nervous and forgot all about it. Forgetting about it is exactly what you have to do.*

**Q** **All this stuff about working through the anxiety's really hard. Isn't there an easier way?**

**A** *Sorry, but the best way I know to get rid of anxiety is to work through it. If you avoid it, it just comes back in triplicate. Remember, as a wise man put it: the greatest weakness of all is the great fear of appearing weak.*

# 14

# The march of age

**Take a look around you. See how our society treats pensioners. Do you want that to happen to you? Make a stand against ageist attitudes.**

*How will you cope when people start talking loudly and slowly at (not to) you?*

Some months ago I had a really bad cold and, by chance, I had to pick up a prescription. I was a bit puzzled when the pharmacist gave me the medicine and laboriously explained what I had to do in words of one syllable but I felt too ill to pay much attention. When I got home I caught sight of myself in the mirror and I realised that the virus had done its work – I looked as though I'd aged ten years overnight. That was when the full horror dawned on me: she'd treated me like an idiot because I looked old.

Is this what we can expect? Well, according to the pensioners I know (particularly the older ones) yes! The older you appear to be, the more you're treated as though you haven't a brain cell left to your name. Don't take my word for it. Have a look around you – even collect ageist comments for a month. Once you tune in to society's view of age you'll be appalled. With some notable exceptions (if you're a politician no one ever seems to mention your age) it's assumed that pensioners are

Here's an idea for you... **Make your voice heard. Take the time to say a public 'thank you' every time you see an example of positive attitudes towards ageing.**

incapable of living any kind of normal life and, if they do, people always seem to be amazed.

It's all very odd. In some societies the older you are the more you're treated as wise and venerable. How can we get that kind of treatment?

I reckon it's simple. We just don't put up with being put down. Now, don't get me wrong. The last thing I want is to start a bloody revolution. There's a right way, and a wrong way of taking a stand. The wrong way is to get militant, and it's wrong because it reinforces existing stereotypes ('grumpy old men'). The right way is to hit 'em where it hurts. One good approach is ridicule – a powerful weapon. Every time you come up against ageism, take the mickey. Put your tongue firmly in your cheek and laugh at their ignorance. If enough of us do it, we'll get the point across.

Or we can go a little further and start a passive revolution...

Defining idea... **'There is one thing stronger than all the worries in the world; and that is an idea whose time has come.'**
VICTOR HUGO

I've seen ads that say things like: 'An exercise routine that avoids the jumping-about that's so bad for the over-fifties.' Hackles raised? Pick a few more examples of blatant ageism to get you in the mood to write your manifesto and you're away. Choose a party name – I like WOW: 'What? Old? Who?'

In the best tradition of revolutionary leaders, you need followers. That shouldn't be difficult because many of your friends are probably about your age. Even if they're looking forward to it, most people approaching retirement are likely to be just as fed up as you are about the potential loss of status it brings.

Invite them all out for the evening. If you've got lots of friends you'd better find somewhere relatively cheap, because when they arrive you need to hand them a large drink. When everyone's suitably chilled out, stand up and proclaim your manifesto. Don't try to make them join up (yet), but challenge them to help you by coming up with great examples of ageism for your banners (or for the website). At the very worst you'll have an entertaining evening, and if they decide to join your Party you might end up making a real difference to our society.

If you're desperate to be able to deal with ageism but lack confidence, try some of the tips in IDEA 20, *Retired people are invisible*.

*Try another idea...*

'You can either be on the stage, just a performer, just going through the lines...or you can be outside it and know how the script works, where the scenery hangs, and where the trapdoors are.'
TERRY PRATCHETT, *Maskerade*

*Defining idea...*

Q **You're right. People do treat me differently now I'm retired. I'm sick of it, but it's hard to laugh when it makes me so mad and I don't have the nerve to start any revolutions. What can I do?**

*How did it go?*

A *Try a more gentle approach. Do the research, know your subject, be ready with your view and have lots of facts to back it up. The more knowledgeable you are about the subject, the less you'll be afraid to point out where they're going wrong.*

**Q   I tried starting a revolution, but I couldn't get anyone interested. What did I do wrong?**

A   *The clue may be in the guy who tried to sell me a mobile phone recently. He could have been the chairman of a multinational company selling eternal youth and my eyes would still have glazed over. I'm not suggesting you're boring, but being a believer yourself isn't always enough to enthuse others. You need fire in your soul to rouse the rabble. Before you start talking, read a women's magazine – where the fifties are merely a time for covering up wrinkles, and women's lives, apparently, cease at sixty. That'll get you going.*

**Q   What can I actually do to encourage a positive attitude to us older people?**

A   *Look for great books and post a review on Amazon; spot articles in the press and write in to the letters page with compliments; find websites that treat people who are retired with dignity and respect and send them a congratulatory email. Just occasionally there's a TV programme that takes it for granted that pensioners are exactly the same people they used to be before they retired. Actively look out for these examples, spread the word about them and even contribute to them if you can.*

# 15

# Don't do it

**Relax. De-stress. In fact, let's go a bit further than that and learn the art of meditation. You've got the time now, right?**

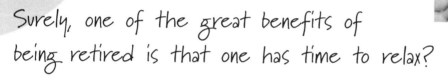

*Surely, one of the great benefits of being retired is that one has time to relax?*

Well, most of my pensioner friends tell me they don't know how they found the time to go to work. I don't know whether they're really busy doing lots of exciting things, or whether Parkinson's Law is taking effect, and household chores are just expanding to fill the time available, but it seems mad to me.

Even if we can avoid falling into the 'busy trap', life's bound to be a bitch. We all have to deal with stress and at any age its potential to make us ill puts it high on the public enemy list. We all know that living with permanently high stress levels can cause all kinds of problems, ranging from debilitating migraines to serious heart disease, but almost worse is its insidious effect on the immune system. You can be so beaten down by long-term stress that you become prey for any nasty bug that's going around, and for autoimmune illnesses where your body, in effect, attacks itself.

When you're faced with a sudden cause of stress (large, salivating dog) or when you're dealing with a continuous stressor (neighbours from hell) your autonomic nervous system sends out complex chemical messages to prepare your body to deal

Here's an idea for you... **Take time to exercise and you'll find you get a triple benefit: you concentrate on something other than your worry; you send lots of great chemicals around your tissues; and you get fitter.**

with the stress. The most famous of these is the 'fight or flight' reaction – hormones are released to make your muscles more efficient. Under continuous stress the hormone cortisol, which normally fluctuates over the course of a day, can stay permanently high.

So what? Well, check out these common symptoms:

■ Comfort eating

■ Increased alcohol consumption

■ Changed sleep patterns

■ Irritability

■ Having lots of minor accidents

■ Frequent minor illnesses

■ Digestive problems (upset stomach, stomach pains, diarrhoea, constipation)

■ Breathlessness or palpitations

■ Thrush or cystitis

■ Mood swings, anxiety, inability to concentrate

Stressed? If you've ticked three or more of these you probably are, so what do you do next? Well, first and foremost, try to get rid of the cause of your stress. Be very specific about

**Keep up the good work with IDEA 38, *Balance the health budget.***

Try another idea…

this, because sometimes the thing you're worrying about, or the thing that's got you into a panic, isn't really the problem. I'll give you a very simple example of what I mean: if you're always stressed about not having enough wine in the house, the underlying cause of your stress could be that you're too far away from the shops, rather than the prospect of an alcohol shortage.

Take some small practical and immediate steps to help yourself (buy a bigger wine rack; cultivate your neighbours). Then, when you've taken the edge off the panic, do some hard thinking about the options available to you (move house, grow vines, drink less).

If you can't remove the cause of your stress altogether, for example if you're caring for an elderly relative, you need to identify some coping strategies. Here are a few to give you a head start:

*'He does not seem to me to be a free man who does not sometimes do nothing.'*
CICERO

Defining idea…

**Get help.** Sounds obvious, but so many people struggle along on their own. There are lots of sources of support, starting with your local council. Sometimes, all it takes is a chat to someone to make you feel better. If you're really desperate and you've no one to talk to, phone the Samaritans.

*'Rest is not idleness, and to lie sometimes on the grass on a summer day listening to the murmur of water, or watching the clouds float across the sky, is hardly a waste of time.'*

SIR J. LUBBOCK, naturalist and archaeologist

**Prioritise.** If you're really busy, work out which tasks can be left for a while – dusting the spare room (dusting anywhere in fact), cleaning the car, phoning Aunt Jane. Then prioritise the ones that need to be done straight away – paying the red electricity bill, feeding the dog, writing a CV.

**Learn to accept the situation.** It may not be fair – life, generally, isn't – but you have to deal with it and that's that.

Make some time for yourself each day, and do something that you find relaxing, whether it's an extra hour's sleep, a couple of chapters of the latest best seller, or half an hour weeding the garden.

**Q**  **I'm much too busy to find time to meditate. What else can I do?**

*A*  *If you really can't find twenty minutes you really are under stress. Read the chapter again and ask yourself whether your tasks are more important than your health.*

**Q**  **OK, maybe I could find a bit of spare time, but I don't see how meditation can help me. Are there any real health benefits?**

*A*  *There are some clear physiological effects from meditation. It slows your heart rate, relaxes your muscles, and those stress hormones are put back in their place for a while. Do give it a try. Find a quiet comfortable spot, close your eyes and meditate. Breathe in slowly and deeply, imagining that the air that's filling your lungs is full of coloured light. Breathe the air out but imagine the light stays. With each successive breath allow the light to expand gradually through your whole body. You may find that the colour of the light changes according to your mood. When you feel completely full of light, allow it to seep back out through your skin so that you are slowly surrounded with an aura of colour. OK, it sounds very hippy, but try it and float on a sea of coloured light.*

How did it go?

# 16

# Earplugs at the ready?

**Because if action really does speak louder than words, you're about to make a lot of noise. Get started on those goals.**

I can just picture you as you read this book. Rubbing your hands with glee at the thought of all the great things you're going to do with your retirement.

Trouble is, life tends to get in the way. You'll want to spend a couple of months just chilling out, getting the feel of your new life. Then there'll be a few odd jobs around the house, and I expect you'll want a holiday, and there'll be Christmas and a New Year celebration…In a year or so you'll find yourself wondering how you ever found time to go to work – and you probably won't be anywhere near doing all the things you'd wanted to do. The best way to avoid this situation is to make your goals really clear and to put some hard edges around them. Here's how.

## SPOT THE BLOCKERS

When you've identified your dreams, do a bit of a reality check. Don't set yourself up for failure. Everest may be unattainable if you're confined to a wheelchair (though I wouldn't bet on it) so spend a bit of time thinking about the things that

Here's an idea for you... **Get a Plan B. Nothing's more frustrating than getting halfway to a goal then finding the world's altered (imagine stealing a million in cash then finding the currency's changed).**

could stop you achieving your ambitions. If there are blockers, is there any way you can get around them?

## LINE UP THE RESOURCES

Think about the resources you might be able to tap into to help you get where you want to be. Who do you know who could help? What skills do you have that will take you part of the way?

## SMART GOALS

There's a knack to scoring goals. You have to set them up properly. I've borrowed a bit of business jargon here: goals should be SMART – specific, measurable, attainable, realistic and timely. So here goes:

'I want to reach Everest base camp by the time I'm 67.' Mmm. OK as far as it goes, but it doesn't go far enough. How are you going to do it?

Defining idea... **'Why, sometimes I've believed as many as six impossible things before breakfast.'**
LEWIS CARROLL, *Alice's Adventures in Wonderland*

'I'm going to book my place on one of the treks, find a fitness course that will prepare me to make the journey, and reach Everest base camp by the time I'm 67.' Much better. This gives you some small steps along the way, so before you know it you'll be halfway to your dream.

'I'll book myself on that course in London, find two people at work to practice on, write a business plan and be ready to set up on my own as an aromatherapist when I retire.' This is good. There's a kind of roller-coaster effect about the kind of plan that opens new

**If your reality check left you feeling bereft, maybe you shouldn't be retiring yet? Flip the pages back to IDEA 3, *Retire to work*.**

*Try another idea...*

pathways and makes some real commitments. Suddenly, you find you're spotting opportunities you'd have missed if you didn't have your ears pricked for 'aromatherapy' and you'll actually be there doing it by the time you retire.

'I want to lose 5 kilos.' Bad example: much better to say, 'I want to be 65 kilos and be able to fit into a size 12 dress.' Why? Because 'losing weight' is pretty negative, whereas 'being 65 kilos' is very positive and uplifting – and you can actually imagine how you'll look in the dress to keep you working towards your goal.

## ACTION PLANNING

And, finally, there's the plan itself. You need to break down your goals into small, easily achievable steps. Warning: don't produce a multi-coloured, many-paged spreadsheet. In our house this is called 'doing a Rimmer' (from the character in *Red Dwarf* who spent so long doing his exam revision planning that he never actually had time to do the revision).

*'Nothing is impossible. There are ways that lead to everything, and if we had sufficient will we should always have sufficient means. It is often merely for an excuse that we say things are impossible.'*
FRANÇOIS DE LA ROCHEFOUCAULD

*Defining idea...*

71

*How did it go?*

**Q** **I'd really love to learn to hang-glide but I'm not super-fit and I'm not getting any younger. At 62, have I left it too late to try?**

A   *Of course not. However fit you are, there's always the chance you won't make this kind of goal (which is why you need a Plan B) but think of the fun you'll have achieving each of those small steps on the way. Remember that the journey matters far more than the destination.*

**Q** **For goodness sake, I've worked for forty years and I'm looking forward to a rest. Why can't I just meander? Why do I need SMART (specific, measurable, attainable, realistic and timely) goals?**

A   *You don't actually need any kind of goals – it's all about what's going to make you happy. When you're on your deathbed and you look back, will you think 'I've had a great time for the last thirty years', or will you wish you'd achieved some long lost dream?*

**Q** **I like the idea of a Plan B as a backup, but I'm having trouble coming up with one that doesn't make me feel a failure. Any pointers?**

A   *Your Plan B can be a simple twist on your original plans, like a move to Country & Western if no one will hire you to sing the Blues, or it can be a different approach (you could write songs instead of singing them). Or you can plan something entirely different. Choose a goal, work out some roughly defined steps to reach it, then put it on the back burner ready to bring to the boil if it's needed.*

## 17

# Get the pasting table out of the attic

**It's not only the wrinkles on your face that age you. Give your home a facelift.**

*Back in the 70s I put loud patterned wallpaper on the walls. In the 80s I hastily removed it. Guess what, it's back! Does your décor date you?*

If you want to keep a young image it's important to keep your home looking good too. I realise, of course, that fashions change because it's in the interests of manufacturers and designers to make them change. Otherwise where would be the market for new furniture and who'd watch all those DIY TV repeats? But now we're looking at a fixed income it's a blasted nuisance isn't it?

I like change. I'm a bit of a shopaholic, so it's no hardship for me to keep spending on the house, but even I get cross when our expensively tiled bathroom suddenly looks dated, so I've decided it's time to get clever about decorating fashions.

*Here's an idea for you...* **Don't forget your floors: buy 80% wool twist pile carpets in a kind of beige-with-black-flecks colour. The carpet will last forever and all marks disappear instantly!**

Are parts of your home looking a bit tired, or even a bit old-fashioned? Before you get the paint and stepladders out of the garage, pretend you're a visitor and look at it all through critical eyes. Review each room for things that look really tired. Ask yourself, do they need a major makeover or can you tart them up?

Once you've got your 'to do' list you're in research mode. You'll need to check what's in style, and that's not difficult because there are zillions of magazines on the subject. Spend a couple of weeks doing some research: cut out pictures of rooms or decorating ideas you particularly like; note down anything that takes your fancy on TV; eye up your friends' houses and decide (privately, of course) what you like, and what you don't like. While you're at it, keep your senses alert for what's in fashion – what shapes, materials, colours seem to be used most at the moment?

*Defining idea...* **'Art produces ugly things which frequently become more beautiful with time. Fashion, on the other hand, produces beautiful things which always become ugly with time.'**
JEAN COCTEAU

When you've done the research, highlight the things you like best; ignore the things you hate. You do, of course, need to avoid extremes (so don't fall for the 'Oh, darling, shocking pink carpet is so *in* this year' hype) but you can adopt the general idea without too much trouble. For example, if loud wallpaper is, for some bizarre reason, back in fashion you can think about papering just one wall; if everywhere is Barbie pink this year, you can decide to buy a few pink accessories. That'll make it clear that, whilst not being a fashion victim, yes, you're still a hip person who has a great sense of style and can successfully adapt the current fashion to her needs. Beware of choosing minimalism though. Brilliant white walls and beech floors need to be accessorised with serious art and megabucks-worth of designer gear or it just looks as though you've moved to a dentist's waiting room.

**If all this decorating has made you thoroughly dissatisfied with your home, have a look at IDEA 24, *Stop swinging that poor cat.***

*Try another idea...*

Now, yippee, it's time to shop. It's OK seeing things on a screen, or in a glossy photo, but (assuming you can find them locally) they might not look quite the same in real life. Colours, textures, price are all crucial and, whatever you do, don't forget to take a tape measure. I know someone who bought a truly great sofa, only to find that the delivery men needed to take out the entire window frame to get the thing into his house.

If you have a kitchen or bathroom on your revamp hit list you'll know prices vary enormously depending on what you choose. If you're not yet retired, think about delaying these larger jobs till you're work-free and can take a bit of time to suss out exactly what you want, and where to get the best bang for your bucks. If you need to get started soon, at least consider delaying till the next sales. When you do choose, avoid anything that's trendy. Remember that avocado bathrooms were the height of cool when they first hit the shops, but it wasn't their trendiness that doomed them – it was their strong statement. I'm willing to bet that Mediterranean-inspired wall tiles, mosaics and beech kitchen units will be tomorrow's signpost for a dated look.

'*It's new fancy rather than taste which produces so many new fashions.*'
VOLTAIRE

*Defining idea...*

*How did it go?*

**Q**   **I disagree with you. OK, neutral is sensible but why do I need to be so boring?**

*A*   *Think of neutral as a cool backdrop for beautiful possessions. Cream walls are an excellent background for great paintings. If you're on a small fixed income and want to do something to your home that'll last for a long time, neutralising the major areas is a really good way to go. Paint the walls and woodwork in one of the fifty shades of cream offered in your local DIY store, or wallpaper in the plainest, palest design you can find. Choose large items of furniture in neutral plain colours, because quirky colours and patterns go out of fashion too quickly.*

**Q**   **My house is OK but old fashioned and I can't afford to revamp it. What can I do?**

*A*   *Why don't you wear retro with pride? We keep seeing revivals of various decades, so whichever yours belongs to, buy a couple of key accessories that are typical of the period and emphasise the point that you've chosen this look deliberately. Keep everywhere ultra-clean and tidy and convince everyone you're the ultimate in chic.*

# 18

# Where's the Enigma machine when you need it?

**Because if you haven't already found out, you'll soon discover when you get your pension forecast that it's in a kind of code. You may need to call in the experts.**

*I reckon pensions are more complex than particle physics — best to be smart and get someone else to do the work.*

Nine out of ten 'retirement' books are really just about pensions – and I've read most of 'em, so making it easy on yourself starts here with a snapshot of what's out there.

## STATE PENSIONS

If you're in the UK and were born before 6 April 1950 you can expect a state pension at 65 (men) or 60 (women) provided you've paid enough National Insurance contributions, or have been credited with them (if, for example, you were sick or unemployed, or receiving maternity allowance or in full-time education). Women be warned: there will be a phased increase of the state retirement age from 2012 (increasing up to 65) which will affect you if you were born after 5 April 1950.

**Before you hire an independent financial adviser, ask how much you'll be charged for the initial interview and for continuing advice. And get quotes from different advisers.**

In addition to the basic state pension, you may be entitled to some additional payments (what used to be SERPS and is now the State Second Pension).

If you're just a few months away from retirement, contact the Department of Work and Pensions to make sure they have your current address and they'll send you a statement.

If you're still a couple of years off retirement age and want to know what to expect, do yourself a favour and don't reach for back payslips and the calculator. There's no point in trying to work it out for yourself when an expert will do it for free. All you need to do is phone your local pension services office and ask them for a Pension Forecast Application Form, known as BR19 to its mates. If you're not in the UK the names and numbers will be different, but a BR19 by another name will smell as sweet. A few weeks later you'll get a written statement of your prospective pension.

It's possible in some (limited) cases to make up a backlog of National Insurance contributions, which will of course increase your pension entitlement. You can also defer your pension for up to five years if you want to continue working after the state pension age, and extra pension will be credited to you for each year you work. Make sure you defer any graduated pension too, or you may lose out.

**Benefits**

If you're in the UK, ring the Pensions Credit Helpline on 0800 99 1234 to find out whether you're entitled to benefits.

Has all this gibberish depressed you? IDEA 1, *Glory days*, might cheer you up.

*Try another idea...*

## PRIVATE PENSIONS

Are you in a private pension scheme? In a quick canter through one pension guide I counted ten, yes ten, different kinds of scheme, so there's no point in my boring you to death with the details. You should be getting an annual statement, but if you want an estimate now, contact the scheme manager and ask for one – and don't be put off by his air of superiority!

## INCREASING YOUR PENSION

It may still be possible to increase your pension entitlement by paying in some Additional Voluntary Contributions. Speak to your pension provider to find out whether it's worth doing this.

## EARLY RETIREMENT

Make sure you're not going to be heavily penalised for retiring early. Pension schemes have a wildly unreasonable prejudice against those who opt for the good life even a couple of years early and will take a huge chunk out of your pension to show their disapproval.

*'I just need enough to tide me over until I need more.'*
BILL HOEST, cartoonist

*Defining idea...*

Defining idea...

*'It is better to have a permanent income than to be fascinating.'*
OSCAR WILDE

## ANNUITIES

Despite lobbying from the pensions industry and the media, the government seems set on managing our retirement income for us, and unless you're in a final salary scheme, you're going to have to buy an annuity at some point in the future. The key thing to remember about annuities is that the insurer who pays you *makes money* – otherwise he wouldn't do it would he? That means you could get more if you were investing your dosh yourself. Grr.

Don't automatically take the advice of your pension provider, because there are vast differences in what you can buy. If you don't think it's worth the effort, just check out annuity rates in one of the broadsheet papers! They'll tell you how much you can get each year if you have £100,000 to invest and you'll be amazed at the differences.

Don't forget to contact ex-employers well before retirement if you didn't transfer your pension entitlement over to your new employer.

**Q**  **I forgot to ask whether retiring early will affect my state pension. Will it?**

*How did it go?*

*A*  *You may need to continue paying National Insurance contributions until you reach state retirement age. Check with the Department of Work and Pensions.*

**Q**  **Do I take the tax-free lump sum?**

*A*  *That depends on whether you prefer cash now, to spend or to invest, or whether you'd rather lump it all into the eventual annuity purchase. You really need to take professional advice on this one because it all depends on your individual circumstances.*

**Q**  **Should I use an independent financial adviser? Are they any good?**

*A*  *Independent financial advisers are heavily regulated professionals, so it's a good idea to find one to help you invest your pension money. Choose someone who's not tied into a product and will advise you on the whole range of options, rather than just a limited selection. By the way, don't be shy about interviewing a few before you choose. This person is going to be crucial to your efforts to live the life of Riley and you want to be dealing with someone you instinctively trust.*

# 19

# VO2 max it

**Whaddya mean you don't understand? Shame on you. Get down and work that body at once.**

## Have you ever wondered why everyone's walking past you these days?

It happened to me a year or so ago, crossing Waterloo Bridge. I've always walked fast and I couldn't for the life of me work out what was happening. Why was everyone sprinting this morning? It took me a while to realise what was wrong. I'd got older. The fitness I'd always taken for granted had slithered away over the years as muscle turned to fat and joints stiffened from lack of use.

It's absolutely true that youth is wasted on the young. I never appreciated the sheer energy I used to have till I lost it. There's no getting away from it, by the time we reach retirement age we have to work a lot harder to stay in the same place. Worse! Because we're not as resilient as we used to be, we need our fitness more than ever. We need it to fight off infection, we need it to keep mobile and, frankly, we need if it we're going to have some fun.

Whatever shape you're in, kick off your exercise programme by checking with your doctor that it's OK for you to step up the pace a little. Don't miss out this step because you could do some serious damage by launching straight into a fitness

*Here's an idea for you...* **If you cringe at the idea of the gym, just build exercise into your lifestyle. Start small. Play music and dance around the lounge when you vacuum; use stairs instead of escalators; tighten your buttocks when you're standing at the sink washing up.**

programme (at the least you risk torn muscles, agonised abs and a grim determination never to exercise again).

Next, be honest about how much exercise you do these days, and assess how you're doing in the three key areas of aerobic fitness, suppleness and strength.

First the exercise. How much time do you spend sitting down, or lying down? Do you use the stairs or do you automatically head for the lift or the escalators? Try using a pedometer to work out whether you're anywhere near the recommended 10,000 steps a day. Do you consciously work out, or have you become a couch potato?

## NOW CHECK YOUR FITNESS

VO2 max is a good measure of aerobic fitness because it's a number, rather than a description of how you feel. It refers to your lung capacity and a fitness trainer can check it for you with a calculation based on a mile walk or run.

*Defining idea...* **'You have to stay in shape. My grandmother, she started walking five miles a day when she was 60. She's 97 today and we don't know where the hell she is.'**
ELLEN DEGENERES

If you're not sure how flexible you are, do a bit of self-watching for a week. Do you suffer from backache or painful joints? Do you groan when you bend (a sure sign of age)? Are there places you just don't attempt to reach any more?

And how strong are you? Do you struggle to lift things these days? Don't win every time at arm wrestling?

Whatever your fitness level, there's no need to look far for get-fit ideas. We're inundated with advice on exercise: adverts for gadgets (the Amazing Super-Dooper Abs Cruncher that will give you a six pack in six weeks at a cost of only half your annual pension), DVD fitness classes with leggy blondes, upbeat TV programmes with oiled bodies, downbeat classes at local schools, hectoring articles in newspapers and even glossy magazines specifically devoted to getting fit. You couldn't get away from it even if you wanted to.

Top tip – if you're extremely unfit, start as gently as possible by taking a walk. Make it a short walk on day one; make it a little longer on day two. By walking a bit more each day you'll improve your cardiovascular fitness and your muscle tone. To complement the walking find an exercise that's slow and controlled so there's no danger of over-stretching your muscles. Try Tai Chi, or a beginners' yoga class, or Pilates. All of these will boost your flexibility and a good teacher will make sure you don't push yourself too hard.

**Is the thought of all that exercise getting you down? Cheer up by reading IDEA 25, Chocolate is good for you.**

*Try another idea...*

'*I take my only exercise acting as pallbearer at the funerals of my friends who exercise regularly.*'
MARK TWAIN

*Defining idea...*

85

How did it go?

**Q** **I joined a gym last September and I've been going three times a week for an hour. I was hopelessly unfit when I started but I was really beginning to feel fitter. Then I slipped and broke my ankle. I haven't been back since and I'm dreading it. What will a six-week break have done to my fitness level?**

*A* *If you were feeling pretty fit before the break you'll probably be surprised at how quickly you regain your pre-break fitness level once you've done with the physiotherapy and can get back to a full gym programme. Mind you, the first couple of sessions are going to be grim, so you might want to cut your hour down to thirty minutes!*

**Q** **I'm not wasting my retirement taking exercise. How can I still keep fit?**

*A* *Buy yourself a resistance band (you can get them in any sports shop) and follow the exercises on the packaging in the privacy of your own bedroom. Make life a bit difficult – get up and turn the TV over manually, make one cup of tea rather than a pot, so you'll have to walk back into the kitchen. Even small changes will improve your fitness.*

**Q** **I hate exercising. When do I get too old to do it?**

*A* *Sorry, but you don't. Research shows that even elderly and infirm people can benefit from increasing their exercise levels.*

# 20

# Retired people are invisible

**People tend to class anyone with lines on their face and a few grey hairs as 'just another old person'. Keep your personality intact. Walk the fine line between passivity and aggression and make sure you're not overlooked.**

*Every day we're faced with some media view of retired people as grumpy old men, meek old ladies, mad professors.*

The biggest problem with these stereotypes isn't that they're wrong (though, of course, they are). No, the problem is that we've all got used to pigeonholing 'pensioners' and we've forgotten that they're individual human beings. This is exactly how we treat young children too – they're all lumped into general categories like 'pre-teen', 'truant', 'under-five'. We forget they're individuals, with unique needs and unique talents.

Sooner or later you'll find you're ignored by the trendy barman out to impress the girls, or talked down to by a baby doctor with a brand new stethoscope around her neck, or overlooked for a place on the village football team because, obviously, you're past it. When that happens you have a choice. You may well feel like retiring

Here's an idea for you... **Lock yourself in the bathroom, turn to the mirror, take a deep breath, square your shoulders and say these words, firmly but quietly (if you're sure you're alone in the house feel free to bellow): I am a grown up; I can say no to unreasonable demands; I can make my own decisions; I have the right to be heard. Repeat as necessary, then take three deep breaths and go to face your challenge.**

hurt, hiding away and pretending a passive acceptance of the injustice. Don't – you'll gradually lose confidence in your abilities if you do that too often. Or you may get cross and start howling 'I don't believe it' – then you'll find yourself angry and disliked. Much better to be assertive, and if you're not a naturally assertive person you can start practising now, so that you're ready for the fray.

The biggest misconception about assertiveness is that it means you get your own way. It doesn't. So what is it? Actually, it's easier to start with what it's not.

It's not aggressiveness: feeling irritable or defensive, or thinking 'This shouldn't happen to me; how dare they?' If you're being aggressive you're behaving badly – for example you'll be shouting, swearing, getting violent or being sarcastic.

Defining idea... **'He who establishes his argument by noise and command shows that his reason is weak.'** MICHEL DE MONTAIGNE

It's not passiveness: feeling depressed or frustrated, or guilty, or thinking 'I'm not important'. Saying 'yes' when you ache to scream 'no'; shrinking quietly into the background when you should be contributing or enjoying yourself.

Incidentally, it's not sulking or backstabbing either – that's being a passive aggressive and is likely to drive other people up the wall.

**Why not go the whole hog and become totally visible? Read IDEA 7, *Don't act your age.***

*Try another idea...*

OK. What does it mean to be assertive? It means being confident, calm and clear and, crucially, it means that everyone walks away feeling OK about themselves. It's a win/win outlook. Yes, you'll need to make compromises, but if you approach people in the right way you'll usually find they'll be willing to make compromises too.

If you know you're about to face a situation where your needs are likely to be overlooked, or just plain stamped on, always remember to PLAN:

- **P**repare your case. Know what you want, and how you feel about it

- **L**isten to what the other person says and let them know you've heard them

- **A**sk the other person to listen to you, and explain what you want, and how you feel

- **N**egotiate a deal that leaves both of you feeling satisfied

*'An angry man is again angry with himself when he returns to reason.'*
PUBLIUS SYRUS

*Defining idea...*

*How did it go?* **Q** **I live in a terraced house and my next-door neighbour insists on having his TV on full blast. I tried what you suggested but he went mad. He says it's none of my business how he watches his TV and he can't hear it if it's quiet – in fact he shouted at me for ten minutes and I got very upset. Is there anything else I can do?**

*A* *Don't give up. Try again, and have a go at a technique called 'fogging', which is very handy when someone's being aggressive. Defuse the situation by agreeing that your neighbour has the right to his point of view. Acknowledge what he's saying – of course he has a right to watch his own TV – but don't budge on your own side of the story. Keep repeating your case over and over again, calmly saying things like 'Yes, I know you enjoy the TV, but I enjoy watching my programmes too, and I find it difficult to hear my own TV when yours is so loud.'*

**Q** **Your comment about saying 'no' really struck a chord with me. John, my brother, keeps asking me to look after his dog. It's getting to be almost every weekend and I'm sick of it. I don't want to hurt his feelings so how can I even suggest I don't want to do it?**

*A* *Remember the win/win formula. Explain that you enjoy Fang's company and don't want to stop having him to stay but, like John, sometimes you'd like to have a dog-free weekend. Suggest that you work out a schedule that gives you both a nice balance between a bit of freedom and the pleasure of having the dog with you.*

## 21

# Don't split hairs

**Now you've left work you can relax on the grooming regime can't you? Well, no. Unkempt hair, torn nails and eau de tramp aren't nice. Have a long, hard look at yourself and make sure you're not displaying bag lady chic.**

*As you enter retirement world, you may need to look for new motivation to keep your grooming standards up.*

You'd think, wouldn't you, that people's motivation to be well groomed would be pretty high when they're working full time? Oh yeah? So how come I've worked with women who leave the loos without first washing their hands (as long as they think there's no one watching)? Yeuk.

OK. That's particularly unpleasant, but everyone's standards slip from time to time. Let's face it, it's lovely to feel fresh and clean, but it's even nicer to slob out occasionally.

But scruffiness can add years to your age. If you don't believe me check it yourself – look in the mirror after a busy day when you haven't had the chance to freshen up. Dull skin, tired eyes, untidy hair – they all add to a general impression of someone who's lost interest, and that impression is ageing. Give yourself a quick facial, wash and condition your hair and you'll see how you can look immediately younger. If a

*Here's an idea for you...*

**Guys, if you bleed every time you shave you're being too harsh with yourself. If you've been using soap or foam all these years, try one of the shaving oils or gels, and feel that razor glide. Or how about booking a session with a professional barber to get some tips on how to do it painlessly?**

quick wash 'n' brush up can make you look better, think how much more effect you'll achieve if you do some serious grooming.

The rules aren't that different, except you need to be a lot more gentle with yourself these days, because skin gets thinner and drier as we age. Of course, you could just be one of life's lucky people with fabulous skin and no wrinkles, but if your skin looks great it's probably because you're doing the right things to it. However, if it looks red, dry, lined or coarse, give it a bit of TLC. You don't have to spend a fortune – you can buy quite cheap skincare products that are unscented and free of detergents – but you do have to use them regularly. You also have to be gentle. Don't scrub your face; stroke it and soothe it.

Cleanse, tone and moisturise. Men don't seem to know about this, though it's been drummed into women for years. Just because you're retired doesn't mean the rule doesn't matter any more. Use a gentle cleanser on your face, followed by an even gentler toner (no alcohol please – and that includes aftershave), topped up by the moisturiser of your choice. Yes, men too.

*Defining idea...*

**'By common consent grey hairs are a crown of glory; the only object of respect that can never excite envy.'**
GEORGE BANCROFT, American writer

Treat yourself occasionally to a facial – either a professional job or a self-applied session of gentle exfoliation, facemask and warm towels to make your skin glow.

Liver spots? There are creams that fade them out. Don't know how they work but they do, as long as you keep up the treatment. I bought a tube once. Saw the ad, strolled along to the beauty counter, handed over the credit card. Almost fainted when I signed the slip and realised how much I'd paid! You have been warned.

If you don't think this goes deep enough, read IDEA 41, *Get an MOT*.

*Try another idea...*

Don't forget the body. Gently exfoliate (or, as my husband insists on calling it, 'defoliate') then moisturise. I have a theory about body lotion, formed after a holiday where I was constantly applying sun cream and ended up with fab skin. Never mind the quality – feel the width. Lots of cheap body lotion works better than skimpy applications of hundred quid a shot stuff.

Hands show your age; feet feel it. My idea of heaven is a pedicure, and if you've never had one I can highly recommend the experience. But in any event you should be treating your extremities with the same care and attention you're going to lavish on the rest of you. Loadsa cream.

Finally, the hair. Is it my imagination or is grey hair rather coarse and brittle? I can personally recommend a henna wax treatment, which leaves your hair feeling ten years softer. Still, that doesn't change the colour. Do I age gracefully or do I bleach? Hmph. I was born blonde and I intend to die blonde. You suit yourself.

And what about baldness? Hair transplants are for the rich; wigs are for the brave. Please believe this: bald can be sexy, so wear the style with pride. On no account should you comb long strands of hair across your bald patch. It looks ridiculous.

'Grey hair is a sign of age, not of wisdom.'
GREEK PROVERB

*Defining idea...*

**Q** **All this beautifying is OK for women but you don't seriously expect me to have a facial do you?**

*A* *Yes. We're in the 21st century and men can do these things. If you've never had a facial you just have to try it – it's bliss.*

**Q** **I reckon you're suggesting I should spend quite a lot of money here. Is there a cheap alternative?**

*A* *Unscented own-brand products are cheaper than the posh stuff. However, if even this is beyond your budget you can make your own beauty products with natural ingredients like yoghurt, banana, papaya – there are lots of recipes on the internet.*

**Q** **My nails are pretty good, but my hands look, well, old. Any tips?**

*A* *The condition of your hands is a dead giveaway. If they're wrinkled, red and coarse they tell people straight away that you're not as young as you used to be. Before you go to bed tonight treat them to a gentle exfoliating cream, wash and dry them thoroughly, then smother them with hand cream (remember: quantity matters more than quality when it comes to creams). Tomorrow, and every day for the next fortnight, apply the hand cream lavishly every hour. Watch with amazement as the years fall away.*

## 22

# Bingo, bowls and the church choir

**Community activities for the retired seem to have got stuck in a time warp. Can we invent something new? Or maybe it's already out there and no one's told us? Well, it's a bit of both actually.**

*Maybe you like bingo, live for bowls and are the best soprano in the neighbourhood. But if you're not, or if that's not enough, what else are you going to do with your social life?*

Do you have the faintest idea of what's available locally? To my surprise, I've found there are a lot more activities than I realised. It's all very odd. They sort of bubble under the surface of community life, and you only get to hear about them by sheer accident.

It all happens when, one idle day, you actually read the local paper and there they are – from stamp collecting to line dancing. If you're like me and lucky enough to have a neighbourhood magazine you'll find even more, though just be warned that

*Here's an idea for you...*

**If you can't find something that sparks your imagination and want to start something yourself, sound out your friends, family and neighbours. If enough of them are keen on your bright idea you can start with a small meeting at home for no cost at all. If it's a success you can organise the next meeting in the community centre and charge everyone a small fee to cover the cost.**

you may have to fortify yourself with a large gin and tonic before you start reading this type of magazine. In my (admittedly limited) experience they all appear to be written by eccentrics with their own idiosyncratic, irritating version of the language. However, if you can grit your teeth and make it to the end without bursting a blood vessel or kicking the cat you'll have a huge number of telephone numbers of local clubs and organisations. If you're not this lucky and you don't have a regular letterbox-full of news about local activities try your council website or – even better – a Google search on local organisations and leisure activities.

When you've got your information, where do you go next if, like me, you've never actually imagined yourself doing any of these things? Any local club worth its salt will welcome new members, and if you're not sure which one to go for try the 'Freshers' Day' approach: collect as many details as you can and visit 'em all. Rate each one on a mix of how welcoming they are, fun-potential, cost, specialist facilities, comfort factor (what's the coffee like?) and level of expertise. Ditch the ones that score lowest.

*Defining idea...*

*'This time, like all times, is a very good one, if we but know what to do with it.'*
RALPH WALDO EMERSON

A good route to getting a new club off the ground is to seek out the local experts. If you're interested in home-brewed beer, find out if there's an evening class on brewing. Check out your local booze seller to see if they know of anything in the area. Find something local that you can use as leverage. Maybe there's a wine-tasting club? They're bound to have some ideas on how you can form a branch and will inevitably supply a good network of keen, alcohol-loving members.

**If all this is a bit too gregarious for you and you fancy chilling, read IDEA 32, *Try an alternative approach.***

*Try another idea...*

Finally, if none of these work out for you, get together with a couple of friends and try a bit of innovation. For example, my maniac brothers once held a lager-tasting test. They chose about forty different lagers, sorted them into some complex league table, and played each of them off – I think it was two lagers at a time, one night a week for an entire year. Blind tasting of course (I think this might have involved someone's wife doing the actual pouring so the lads didn't know what they were drinking). Every time I've told people this story they've been keen to copy the idea and I wouldn't be surprised if you managed to set up a national league.

**'Dost thou love life? Then do not squander time, for that is the stuff life is made of.'**
BENJAMIN FRANKLIN

*Defining idea...*

**How did it go?**

**Q** **I'd love to get a few people together to form a jazz band. Any ideas?**

**A** *If you have a music shop locally they probably have a list of music tutors. Contact them to find other people of the same standard as you.*

**Q** **I joined an amateur dramatics group last month but it's very cliquey and I feel thoroughly uncomfortable around them. Shall I just give it up as a bad job and try something else?**

**A** *It's early days yet, so why not persevere for a bit longer? Sometimes the people in these groups need you to work a kind of initiation phase, particularly if most of them have been members since Noah was a lad. They probably want you to make the tea, sweep the stage, paint the scenery and hem the costumes before they accept you as one of their own. Accept the menial jobs for a while, then press for something more exciting.*

**Q** **I've got a range of interests, but I need something to reinvigorate my enthusiasm. Any ideas?**

**A** *Do you have a qualification in any of your interests? What about running a course on it? Take a quick straw poll to find out how much interest there's likely to be – if the ladies down the pub jeer, and the lads in your salsa class look pityingly at you when you suggest a pensioners music class, maybe you should have a rethink. But if they all start talking about forming a brass band you'll have a good chance of persuading a local community centre to give it a go. They run courses on pretty much anything these days and may be really interested in what you can offer them.*

# 23

# Only the lonely

**There's nothing sadder than someone struggling alone, unnoticed. Unless it's two lonely people living yards away from each other and never speaking. Build yourself a network of new friends.**

Somehow, by the time you're reaching retirement age, you feel you should already have lots of friends and a cracking social life, but this isn't always so.

Perhaps you're divorced or bereaved, or maybe you've never found that perfect mate we all dream about. It could be that you've worked abroad all your life and left all your friends behind when you retired back home to an entirely new life. Whatever the reason, it's not too late to do something about it. There's no reason why anyone should be lonely.

It's common sense that if you live on a quiet remote island you're less likely to make new friends than if you live in a busy village but, oddly enough, the reverse isn't true. If you live in the centre of a busy big city it's going to be harder to meet new people than if you're out in the quiet suburbs. But, wherever you live, you won't meet anyone unless you're prepared to work at it.

Here's an idea for you... **If you're planning to use your hobby to play the mating game, find an activity that genuinely interests you – otherwise you'll give up before you even begin – but decide carefully. And have a preview session to see what the gender mix is.**

First and foremost, you won't get anyone to be interested in knowing you if you don't make an effort to be an interesting person and you struggle to find something to say when a new acquaintance asks, 'So, what do you do then?' Do your prep. Be interested in what's going on in the world; have an opinion about current events; have lots of hobbies (even if they sit neglected in cupboards for the greater part of the year, you can still wheel them out if needs be).

Secondly, and I know this is going to sound corny but I have to say it, join a club. Or find something that you enjoy doing and book a course in it. Attend your neighbourhood social activities, or your local church, or get some voluntary work in a local charity shop. Get a job that'll get you into a new environment – it doesn't have to be full time, exciting or even permanent but if it's the right kind of job you'll meet new people.

OK, those are the easy and obvious bits. Much harder, of course, is the actual friend-making bit. How do you make that first, crucial contact? Do you stumble over the first move in case you're rejected? If so, remember that it helps to ask an open question (one that needs more answer than a 'yes' or 'no'). Try something friendly and easy like 'How are you managing to look so cool in

Defining idea... **'The human heart, at whatever age, opens only to the heart that opens in return.'**
MARIE EDGEWORTH, writer

this heat?' If he or she likes the look of you they'll find something to say in response; if they don't, well, just tell yourself that rejection isn't life threatening, and move onto someone else.

**Living the life of a hermit in the wilds? Read IDEA 47, *Location, location, location,* and reassess your priorities.**

*Try another idea...*

When you come to think about it, what exactly is it that makes you warm to people? Of the friends you've had over the years, what was it that attracted you to them? They might have been fun, witty, clever or kind, but I'll bet the one thing they'll all had in common was that they were interested in you. They wanted to know about you – where you lived, what you did with your time, what you enjoyed, what you didn't enjoy.

We don't make friends with people who aren't interested in us, and that's the key to making new friends. Fair do's, you have to be prepared to tell them a bit about yourself, and you have to make sure you're doing those interesting things with your life, but what will really get their eyes alight is your interest in them. Find out what makes your new acquaintance tick, what they do, who they are, and what they think of the world we live in. Watch out though – there's a fine line between being really interested and being intense. Too much interest makes people feel a bit hunted and you don't want a reputation as a stalker!

*'A friend is a gift you give yourself.'*
ROBERT LOUIS STEVENSON

*Defining idea...*

How did
it go?

**Q** **I've joined a couple of local activities and made lots of new friends, but I really want someone special. How can I find love?**

*A* *I think the best kind of love starts with friendship so if you're already making new friends you never know, you could already have met Mr Right.*

**Q** **I can't afford to go out every night, even if I wanted to face the weather, but I get lonely and bored during the long winter evenings and end up stuck in front of the TV. What can I do?**

*A* *Don't think you're alone there! We all do a bit of that in the winter. How about taking an Open University course? You'll be too busy to worry about being bored or lonely – and you'll make new friends too.*

**Q** **There's so much choice of things to do in my neighbourhood. Where's the best place to find a soulmate?**

*A* *Raise the odds of finding love by choosing the right activity. Ladies, how can you possibly hope to meet the love of your life if you spend your evenings with a bunch of women in the body-pump class? Guys, are you going to find real love in your local? Dr Phil McGraw has a wonderful phrase on his TV show – he tells lonely people to find a 'target-rich environment' (OK, so he's borrowed this from the military, but don't let that put you off).*

# 24

# Stop swinging that poor cat

**There are better ways of working out how much space you need in your home now you're retired. In fact, there are probably better ways of using the space you've got.**

All this business of retiring to some tiny cottage by the sea, or a roses-round-the-door thatched job in the countryside — well it's madness.

I don't know anybody who thinks they've got enough space, so unless you're a millionaire I'll bet you feel the same. It was OK for our grandparents – the most exciting retirement activity they had was eating so all they needed was a gas ring. It's different for us: we've got toys. Where are you going to keep yours? If you live with someone, how are you going to cope with the imminent fight for territory? What will it be? Your bike in bits, or his tomato seedlings strewn across the kitchen floor?

This is one of those dull times when you need to make a list. Think of all the basic functions of your home. Include somewhere to eat, places to sleep for everyone, and every leisure activity you can think of that's carried on. Don't forget that

*Here's an idea for you...*

**Look out for one of those amazing Tardis-like cupboards. They look just like an ordinary cupboard, but when you open them they unfold like a Chinese puzzle, full of little nooks and crannies to store all your bits and pieces.**

retirement will give you more time to play, so you need to include the things you want to do as well as the things you're already doing. Obviously there are going to be some interests you don't yet know about – you might suddenly develop a fascination with indoor cricket – but you'll have to deal with that kind of thing when it arrives.

Oh, and you'd be wise to ask any other inhabitants of the house to contribute, or you run the risk of all-out war when your logical analysis allocates the space currently used for your son's computer games to your new unicycle.

Next you need to match activities to space. Draw a rough diagram of your home or, if you're a whiz with those neat computer programs (you know, the ones that draw out your floor plan, fit the furniture in and even paper the walls for you) that'd be great.

Start by putting the fixed activities into place – the ones you can't avoid and that you can't sensibly carry out anywhere else. Be a bit creative here. Obviously, you can only bath in a room with a bath, but you can sleep in pretty well any room that'll hold a bed and you can eat anywhere (even in the bath if you're really desperate for space). The objective is to use as few rooms as possible for these basic activities and to leave as much spare space as you can for playing. Then take it to another level – think about the times you're most likely to be doing those basic activities and make a note of when each space is 'unoccupied'. Don't laugh. If you're creative even the bathroom can have multiple uses – wine making for instance.

Next on the list are the rooms you've always thought of as 'fixed', like your dining room or, even better, that guest bedroom which is used by guests on fewer than half a dozen occasions each year. Mine's nothing more than a luxury hotel for my cat. Assuming I can pluck up the courage to face down the moggie, that's a whole extra room available for about 1,800 hours a year.

Hey presto! With a bit of luck most of us have least one unused room, and all of us should have space in at least one room that's free for a good part of each day. Now all you've got to do is work out what activities can be fitted into each bit of your home.

If your garden is getting you down, read IDEA 50, *Lawn today, lawn tomorrow*, and decide how to cut down the work.

*Try another idea...*

*'Have nothing in your houses that you do not know to be useful or believe to be beautiful.'*
WILLIAM MORRIS

*Defining idea...*

107

**Q**  **I've planned, tidied, decluttered and generally done my best to make space, but I still need more and I really don't want to move. Any ideas?**

**A**  *The obvious answer is to use even more of the space you have. Start by looking up – can you use the space over your head? Is there room for some high shelves? Could your grandchildren sleep in bunk beds, or even on blow-up mattresses? If that doesn't work, maybe you've got a bit of spare space outside? If so, consider having an extension built, or a conservatory, or even a shed. If outside space is at a premium, how about chucking all the junk out of the loft and putting down some cheap flooring?*

**Q**  **Well thanks. I've made space for my sewing and my partner's car gear but now it's driving me mad because it just sits there looking untidy. Where can I put this?**

**A**  *Tackle your messiest room first. Empty it of everything that's easily moveable, look at what's left and ask yourself three questions. Have I used it this year? Is it in good condition? Do I like it? Three 'no's' mean bin it at once. If there's only one 'no', stick it back in the room. Bundle everything else into a spare room and leave it there. You're only allowed to bring things back if you need to use them or if you realise you love them so much you can't bear to be without them. Give it six months then get rid of everything left in the spare room.*

## 25

# Chocolate is good for you

**(Well, as long as it's not your staple diet.) Ditch the supplements and start to eat the kind of food your body really needs to keep it healthy.**

Our body cells renew themselves at an amazing rate and they don't run on thin air. Their regeneration depends on the foods we eat and the liquids we drink, so we need to give them the best raw material we can manage.

If you're like me there was a time, when you were young and had a body working at top efficiency, when you did a fair bit of cheating on the diet front. Don't know about you, but that luxury has long gone for me, and as I've got older it's become less and less easy to get away with mistreating my body. It's not just that pounds pile on overnight and skin looks grey and tired if I eat badly – other things go wrong too (like high blood sugar, low iron levels and furred arteries).

Unfortunately it's not all that easy to treat one's body right. Nutrition is really complicated. Speaking as an amateur, how do I know what's a healthy diet? Here are some food facts:

*Here's an idea for you...*

**Make a 'bingo card' with 72 squares, and in each square write the name of a food item. Each item must only appear once on the card. Rows one and two are for starchy and sugary foods (bread, pasta and cakes). The remaining rows are for vegetables, fruits, dairy, fats and protein foods. Include things you don't usually eat. Tick off as many items as you can in a fortnight. Sheer economics may mean you won't yell 'House' but the challenge is irresistible.**

Eggs are full of cholesterol and you shouldn't eat too many.

Oops, sorry no, dietary cholesterol is OK. It's dietary fat you should avoid.

Oh, sorry again, my mistake. Some dietary fats are fine. Just avoid saturated fats.

Blast. Forgot to say, saturated fats are better than trans fatty acids.

Well, I don't need to go on do I? Advice on nutrition changes with bewildering speed (and from guru to guru). And I'm heartily sick of news headlines that tell me yet another beloved food is bad for me. So what should we be eating for a healthy retirement?

After listening to all the gurus and reading all the contradictions, I've come to the conclusion that it's all about breadth. If you munch your life away on burgers, pizzas, kebabs and chips, and only drink beer or cola, you're going to be seriously malnourished. But if your diet consists of fruit juice, rice, mushrooms, green beans and chicken (perhaps with the occasional doughnut to prove you're still alive), you're probably still in trouble.

Let's say that green beans have plenty of vitamin K; mushrooms have plenty of vitamin B2; and rice has B1, B3 and iron. I devoutly hope that doughnuts have something useful in them too, but I haven't risked looking it up in case they don't. We need all of the right vitamins and minerals to build our new cells, so (ignoring the doughnuts) we obviously can't live on a diet made up entirely of green beans; or of mushrooms; or of rice. Or even of all three since they don't contain enough of the other nutrients we need.

**The obvious next step is IDEA 12, *Chocolate is bad for you.***

Try another idea...

To get the right nutrients we just have to follow the Variety Diet and eat as wide a range of foods as possible. Yes. I know it's stupid and simple. *But it's also brilliant.* Nothing is banned, and variety is king. You can include chocolate, pizza, burger – anything you like – as long as you also include enough different kinds of foods to get the whole range of vitamins and minerals (plus fibre, protein, etc., etc.) that your body needs.

That's all there is to it.

Oh, by the way, from what I can make out spinach does seem to have just about everything in it, so Popeye was right – you probably *could* live on it but, quite apart from the fact that the stuff's disgusting, I foresee some horrible digestive side-effects.

*'No man in the world has more courage than the man who can stop after eating one peanut.'*
CHANNING POLLACK, writer and lyricist

Defining idea...

How did
it go?

**Q** **If I follow the Variety Diet can I be certain it will give me the Recommended Dietary Allowances?**

*A* *I'm not a nutritionist. The diet is just my way of trying to work through a bewildering maze of constantly changing advice in the most sensible way possible. I can't get my head around RDAs or, what I understand to be their successors, Dietary Reference Intakes. Incidentally, the latter give you EARs (yes, really) or Estimated Average Requirements, AIs, or Adequate Intakes, and ULs or Tolerable Upper Intake Levels (I guess they thought TUIL was an acronym too far).*

**Q** **I know you said I should ditch the supplements, but I'm worried about osteoporosis. Surely I should take something extra to avoid this kind of risk?**

*A* *Good question. As I write this there are media articles that suggest you shouldn't. By the time you read this I have no doubt the advice will have changed. I strongly suggest that you should talk to your doctor if you're worried you aren't getting adequate nutrients to manage a current health problem or to avoid a future one.*

**Q** **I've been diagnosed with diabetes. Will eating a varied diet help?**

*A* *Your first port of call for dietary advice if you're diabetic is your doctor, or a specialist nurse. Obviously, your sugar levels are important, and what you eat needs to reflect this. You may find you have to cut some things down, but in general, variety is still good. There are several good cookery books for diabetics if you need some foody inspiration.*

# 26

# If you think you're stressed now...

**Retiring doesn't banish stress – it just brings a whole new lot of things to stress you out. This is bad news (especially at your age!) so when it happens you need to be able to manage it.**

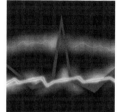

What exactly is stress? It's the adverse reaction people have to excessive pressure, or to other types of demands placed on them.

In other words, it's not the pressure, it's the way you react to it.

How do you know if you're suffering from stress? Well, there are loads of symptoms, but the most common ones (tick 'em off) are:

- Muscle pains (from the tense shoulders and clenched fists)

- Stomach pains (your stomach tenses too)

- Digestive problems (ditto)

- Disturbed sleeping patterns

Here's an idea for you... **Make a wish list that includes all the things you enjoy. You know – the things you say 'I never have time for...these days.' There's a good chance that many of them will only take you half an hour, so make an appointment with yourself – write it in your diary.**

- Over- or undereating

- Headache and migraine

- Irritability

- Crying

- Feelings of anxiety

Have you noticed that some people suffer more from stress than others? It's not just because they're busier (well, not usually). It's because of the type of person they are. Do you know someone who's totally laid back? Do you wish you were like him – or does he irritate the hell out of you? If you just want to drop a grenade in front of him (and even then he probably wouldn't turn a hair) you're like me. We've got a problem. We're called 'type A' and, unlike our Easy Rider 'type B' friends, we're always in a rush. We're competitive, impatient, fast and hard-driving. We, more than anyone else, are likely to miss the warning signs that stay 'Stop, you've gone too far' – and we risk ending up exhausted and burnt-out. How do we deal with it?

Defining idea... **'Do not anticipate trouble, or worry about what may never happen. Keep in the sunlight.'**
BENJAMIN FRANKLIN

We can prevent ourselves from becoming over-stressed, or we can cure ourselves when we get there and, as always, prevention is heaps better than cure. Prevention means watching for the symptoms that suggest you're beginning to slip away from your peak performance level onto the slippery slope of stress – if you're finding it difficult to relax, if you're irritable, if you can't concentrate, ask yourself what's stressing you and do something about it now.

Left it too late? Ideally you should get out of the stressful situation, particularly if your symptoms are severe, but if you really can't do that, try one of these techniques:

**Too stressed to think straight? Read IDEA 28, *Doing the crossword isn't enough.***

*Try another idea...*

Handle the stress in a different way. This might sound impossible, but if you're creative there are usually ways of getting help. Have another look at priorities to see what can be ignored for a while. Or what about getting deadlines changed? I'm often irritated to find that someone's unbreakable deadline just means they're going on holiday tomorrow and want to clear their desk. And what about this statement: not everything has to be perfect. True! Sometimes you can get away with eighty percent.

Distract yourself. I know when I get seriously stressed I forget there's an 'off' switch. I wake up at 2.00 a.m. and worry – as if that ever helped. (I once thought I had the answer to some work problem in the middle of the night, and leapt out of bed to write it down on a scrap of paper. When I read it the next morning I found I'd written utter gibberish.) Book things into your diary that will make it impossible for you to think about whatever is stressing you out – anything will do as long as it takes all of your concentration.

*'Where everything is bad it must be good to know the worst.'*
FRANCIS H. BRADLEY, philosopher

*Defining idea...*

Relax. I know it's very hard, particularly for you Type As, to make time for relaxation when you're stressed. Somehow, it feels like a betrayal ('I can't relax because I'm too stressed. If I relax and de-stress I won't feel like me'). Start small. Even you can lock yourself in the bathroom and sit quietly with your eyes shut for five minutes. Do that five times a day for a week. Next week, take a ten-minute walk every day. The week after you can join the half-hour daily relaxation programme.

*How did it go?*

**Q**  **After a recent heart attack I followed your advice but now I'm so bored I could scream. Help! What can I do to make life more interesting?**

*A*  *We all need some stress – positive stress is what keeps us alive. Check with your doctor to see whether you can resume some of your old activities and, if it's too soon, whether you can try something new that will stretch you a bit without risking your health. And why not contact other heart patients in your area and start a self-help group?*

**Q**  **I'm retired but my partner is desperately overworked and obviously very stressed. How can I help him?**

*A*  *First and foremost, you can be there for him. Be a shoulder to cry on, a rock to lean against. Keep home life stimulating and interesting – change things around a bit just to take his attention off work (but don't go too far or he'll go mad when he can't find his socks). Try to make sure he gets plenty of physical activity. Drag him with you to the gym, convince him he needs a walk before bedtime to help him sleep, get sexy.*

# 27

# A brand named 'old'

**Teenagers are punks with multiple piercings one year, Goths with black eyeliner the next, and then elegant Romantics! But old people are always just old people. Why? Find out, and avoid becoming a stereotype.**

I blame the media and its obsession with the cult of youth.

They worship the ever-changing tides of teen-based fashion, and they show us a hugely diverse (though always thin) population of young to middle-aged adults, but when they get around to including 'old' people (particularly pensioners) what happens? It's that grumpy old sod in the tweed jacket again, or the daft old bat who wanders around the streets in her nightie.

Yet, despite the bizarre views of the media, we all know that it's not just teenagers who change their style. Adults change over the years, as I'm sure you'll agree if you think back to your waist-length hair, bell-bottoms and Quo-obsession back in the 70s (OK maybe not exactly an obsession, but admit it, you did that hands-on-hips dance, didn't you?).

*Here's an idea for you...* **Ready to rock with the iPod but don't have time to search through the dross for the best downloads? Teenagers spend half their lives listening to online music, so ask any relative aged 13–19 to play you his or her two favourite tracks and get a short cut to the latest and best.**

I guess the problem is that there are lots of retired people who actually do fit into the media stereotype. Avoid this at all costs. If you're tempted to let your standards slip and buy something dreary like flannel underwear, just remind yourself that you're a baby boomer (one of the originals, not the 70s boomers who are, in reality, nothing more than our kids trying to get in on our act). You have a reputation to uphold! The world has revolved around us since we were born and there's no reason why that should stop.

Here are my instant hints for keeping the world on its toes.

First and foremost, get the clothes right. At all costs avoid the two extremes – odd assortments of old clothes you used to go to work in, or gear that's so neatly starched, pressed and buttoned that people will think you're an android. Both extremes will scream 'old person'. Jeans. Guys, please, unless you've retained the figure of the guy in the Levi's laundrette ad, don't wear them. They make you look *sooo* dated (and rolls of fat over the belt don't help at all). Ladies, you're not escaping free of criticism. Hipsters with crop tops are for thin teenagers who really don't (apparently) feel the cold when they're showing six inches of midriff in mid-January.

Watch the accessories too. Keep 'em stylish – you don't have to resort to check caps or plastic rain hoods to keep warm and dry. It's probably unreasonable of me, but I also have a deep personal prejudice against men who use those little leather purses. Get a debit card for goodness' sake.

**If you're desperate to be more stylish and want to revamp your wardrobe, have a look at IDEA 34, *Get into the closet.***

*Try another idea...*

Of course, it's not just what you wear – what you do and how you behave sends a message to the world about who you are. I admit to a sneaky liking for the idea of a tour bus full of ancient baby boomers singing 'I can't get no satisfaction' at the top of their voices, but this doesn't mean you should get stuck in a musical time warp. Keep up to date and make sure you download at least two new tracks a week onto the MP3 player (which, natch, you'll be wearing while you're working out at the gym).

Moods and attitudes, too, are a dead giveaway. Express your personality by all means, but avoid the twin nightmares of grumpiness and eccentricity unless you want to step out of character to make an occasional point.

I could go on but I think you get the picture. Avoiding the 'old' brand is very simple – you just need to keep evolving – give it your all, all the time. The minute you begin to avoid change you stop growing and you enter the dim twilight years of grey cardigans, blue rinses and Roll Out the Barrel.

*'Everyone thinks of changing the world, but no one thinks of changing himself.'*
LEO TOLSTOI

*Defining idea...*

*How did it go?*

**Q    I like myself the way I am! Why should I change?**

A    *If you don't care that people think of you as 'just another old person' go ahead and try to stay the same, but the bottom line is that change happens whether you want it to or not. If you get comfortable you can bet your life that something will come along and tip you over. In my view it's better to meet it halfway and choose the direction of change, rather than have it forced on you and end up not liking yourself at all.*

**Q    What's wrong with being eccentric?**

A    *The problem is this: being young-and-eccentric gets you noticed. People will think 'How radical; how cool' or, at worst, 'How silly. Aah but she's young, she'll grow out of it.' Being old-and-eccentric just means people think you're dotty.*

**Q    It's hard work getting out of a rut. Do I really have to bother?**

A    *It's important to keep up to date, but I agree it takes energy. Avoid procrastination by pre-booking a trendy date with yourself once a month. Don't plan too far ahead (in case something new and tempting turns up in a couple of months' time) but block out dates in your diary, buy tickets, book tables, buy magazine subscriptions so that everything's lined up to make it easy. It doesn't matter what you choose – you could go to see a new film (yes, the latest Harry Potter counts), read one of the year's Booker nominations, you could even plan to watch MTV for the evening as long as it's not a nostalgia channel.*

## 28

# Doing the crossword isn't enough

**(Especially if it's in the same newspaper every day.) You want to stay sharp and alert till the day you die, so how many ways can you find to stretch your mind and keep those brain cells working?**

*Our minds deteriorate as we age, right? Brain cells die off at a frightening rate of knots and our memories fade once we hit thirty, OK?*

Not right. Not OK. The latest research is really encouraging. It finds that we can do a lot to make sure our brains can stay fit and healthy, our minds sharp and active and our memories intact by keeping our bodies fit and healthy and by getting plenty of mental stimulation.

Staying fit and healthy is one thing, but what kind of mental stimulation should we be getting? If you do the crossword in *The Times* every day and you get faster at doing it, does that mean you're getting the mind-bending your brain needs to keep it fit? Perhaps it even means you're getting cleverer each day? No, it doesn't.

*Here's an idea for you...* **If crosswords and word games bore you, try Sudoku. It could be just the thing to flex your brain a little. Many newspapers now have a daily game of this, and there are plenty of Sudoku websites now.**

What it means is you've got used to the newspaper's style, you recognise the format and your brain has laid down a pattern for completing the crossword. The more often you follow the pattern, the deeper it becomes etched.

So what? Well, the problem here is that we're basically lazy creatures – our brains try to use existing patterns if they can, so yours will try to use *The Times* crossword pattern to do the crossword in any other paper. Sometimes, it'll work (there are, after all, only so many varieties of crossword). Sometimes, however, you'll come up against a fiendishly different crossword and you'll be lost. The pattern is useless. So you're not cleverer, you're just in a *Times-crossword-habit*.

To keep your mind active you have to keep your brain on its toes (if you see what I mean). That means you have to make it form new connections, lay down new neural pathways. How? Simple. Push the boundaries. Every day, do something different. It really doesn't matter what it is. Learn something new, try something unusual to eat, walk a different way to the corner shop, read a politician's autobiography, or a history book, visit a gallery. Do anything that makes you think.

*Defining idea...* **'TV is chewing gum for the eyes.'**
FRANK LLOYD WRIGHT

Here's something different for you to try straight away. Spend the next ten minutes working out as many ways as possible of using a paper clip.

Done it? OK. Now spend ten minutes working out fifty ways of using a broomstick.

You may be surprised to find that you did better on the second challenge than you did on the first. That's because you had a target to aim at with the broomstick task, and we humans seem to take an almost perverse pride in reaching targets, so one good way of stimulating your brain is to set yourself a daily target. It can be pretty much anything you fancy. My target today is to write a first draft of four of these chapters. What's yours?

Does memory deteriorate as you age? Well, mine's always been useless, but whatever your age, learn to compensate by using this simple trick. Let's imagine you're rushing to catch a plane and you remember five things you have to do when you get back home again.

**Stimulate your mind even more with IDEA 22,** *Bingo, bowls and the church choir.*

*Try another idea...*

*'It is not enough to have a good mind. The main thing is to use it well.'*
RENÉ DESCARTES

*Defining idea...*

Here's an idea for you...
You don't have time to make a list because you'll barely make the check-in deadline, so you need to keep all five things in your head until you're safely on board and can find pen and paper. Here's the list:

- Buy coffee

- Order flowers for your mother-in-law's birthday

- Pay the phone bill

- Phone the bank

- Clear the leaves from the front path

You won't have time to write till you're settled down, so an obvious trigger will be the action of buckling your seat belt. That'll jog you into finding your pen – and if you get distracted you'll be touching the belt again during the journey, so there will be other opportunities to remember.

Now imagine that as you fasten the buckle it erupts into a bunch of flowers. They burst across the cabin where your mother-in-law, dressed as a stewardess, collects them and drops one flower and one crispy brown leaf into a cup of coffee on her tray. She hands you the coffee and a bill, then phones the bank to check your credit rating. Easy!

**Q** **I'd love to do a degree, but I'm now in my mid-sixties. Do you think I've left it too late?**

*How did it go?*

**A** *Certainly not. Loads of people your age are doing degrees. Check out the Open University and the University of the Third Age – both offer a huge range of subjects and a flexible and supportive learning programme.*

**Q** **I can feel my brain seizing up from lack of use. What can I do?**

**A** *Get your brain working away by learning something new and interesting. If you're nervous about learning again after all these years you can begin with something light-hearted and fun, like flower arranging or wine tasting. If you feel a little braver, take the plunge and choose a subject that's right outside your comfort zone. How about training to be a tour guide, learning a language, or taking a vocational subject that might get you a new job? Anything that's different will be a great way of stimulating your brain cells.*

**Q** **I've worked as a statistician all my life and I'm sick of using my brain. Can't I just switch off?**

**A** *This isn't a problem, because as long as you're learning it doesn't have to be 'academic'. Learning to do anything is stimulating for the brain, so you could take up carpentry or hang-gliding if that's what you fancy.*

# 29

# Eating the elephant

**Obviously, you do it one bite at a time, which is exactly how you deal with major problems.**

I don't know why it is — and I guess you'll agree with me on this — but troubles have an evil habit of piling up, one on top of another, leaving us desperately trying to work out which one to deal with first.

No matter how capable we are there's a limit to how many problems we can manage at one time.

I'm not talking about emergencies – if you're facing a crisis situation, the issue usually resolves itself. Priorities become very clear and your mind goes into self-preservation mode, dealing with each necessary task as it arrives. No, I'm talking about the situation where you're already facing a whole heap of problems and then another deadline arrives, and you don't know what to tackle first.

*Here's an idea for you...* **Ask a trusted friend what she or he thinks is the task that you ought to prioritise. You may well not agree, but a different perspective can be useful if you've been stuck obsessing over your plight for a while.**

If you're in this position, try not to procrastinate (if you ever see me ironing you'll know I'm desperately avoiding a heap of deadlines). Obviously it doesn't get you anywhere, and you'll feel even more stressed when you get back to the problems.

Instead, begin by giving yourself some space and some privacy, so you can think quietly about what you have to face and the immediate priorities. Work out what must be done, what can be delayed, where you might get help. If you're the kind of person who works best with a list (or even if you aren't) write down your tasks in order of importance, and then calmly tackle one at a time, giving each your full concentration.

That's hard if you're a worrier, always thinking about the next problem. When the world's on your shoulders it's all too easy to spend all your energies agonising over the future. Endless hours are passed away imagining how it will be. Will I be able to finish this in time? What will he say? How will I reply? You rehearse conversations around your head. (Was any imaginary conversation ever helpful, I wonder? These things never turn out the way you'd expected them to.) Meantime you're not giving your full attention to the job in hand.

*Defining idea...* **'The waste of life occasioned by trying to do too many things at once is appalling.'**
ORISON S. MARDEN, American writer

If you're like that – the kind of person who's bathing her baby grandson and worrying about whether he's going to go to sleep when you put him to bed – you can stop the worrying in its tracks by one simple exercise. Remind yourself that worrying's not doing any good, because your internal thoughts won't help him doze off, and then ask yourself 'What's the worst that can happen, and how would I deal with it?' Work out some ways of coping with

IDEA 10, *Where there's a way…there's a will*, might get you over some of your long-term worries.

Try another idea…

that worst-case scenario. If the baby doesn't sleep you can play with him, or sing to him, or even ring his parents and get them back from the theatre. OK that'd be embarrassing but it's hardly the end of the world. Then get back to living in the here and now. Get on with his bath and have some fun.

This kind of thing's even worse, if you're a multi-tasker. (Men, that means doing more than one thing at time. Don't worry, this is something most of you can't do, so you can skip this bit.) For years I took a positive pride in never doing one thing when I could be doing two. One day one of the secretaries suddenly went ballistic. 'Why do you always carry on typing when I'm talking to you? Why do you never listen to me?' I hadn't even realised I was doing it. I was so anxious not to waste a second that I was tackling two things, doing each badly, and I lost a friend as a result.

The key to inappropriate multi-tasking is to get things in perspective and sort out your priorities before you begin. You're probably not doing either job as well as you could and the world won't end if one job gets done later than the other. While I'm on the subject, can I make a particular plea here? Girls, don't put your mascara on while you're waiting in a traffic jam. It terrifies the rest of us.

*'It ain't no use putting up your umbrella till it rains.'*
WILLIAM RALPH INGE, author and clergyman

Defining idea…

*How did it go?*

**Q** **I don't just have one major problem. My father, who lives a couple of hundred miles away, is very ill. My wife's been made redundant and she's obviously very depressed, and just to make it perfect my new boss is a pig and I'm hating my job. I'm feeling desperate. What do I do?**

**A** *It's natural that you want to support your wife and your father, but you'll be no help to them if you crack up yourself. Give them whatever support you can, but remember to look after yourself too. Try to schedule some 'me time' every day, and if you can't find that time how about talking your problems through with a counsellor or a life coach?*

**Q** **I'm struggling to concentrate on what's important. Have you got any techniques that might help me?**

**A** *Try living for the whole of today at one hundred percent – it's curiously comforting. If you think a whole day is too much to tackle, you can start small. Decide what you want to do now, this very second. Do nothing else except that. If it's eating a slice of toast, give your full concentration to the experience. No TV, no radio, no newspaper, no conversation, no nothing. Just a thick slice of hot, buttered toast. Savour the delicious taste, enjoy the smell, feel the texture in your mouth. Yum.*

# 30

# Kids' stuff

**Are your children still on your hands? Or are you on theirs? This one's about how to manage the changing relationship between you and your offspring once retirement is reality. Oh, you don't think it'll change? Just wait and see!**

*It's important to get that relationship with your kids right when you retire, or you'll end up feeling resentful in one of three different ways. What do I mean?*

## SICK OF SHELLING OUT

You're retiring early, or you delayed having children until relatively late in life, and you're facing a couple of major issues. First and foremost, obviously, there's the cost involved in keeping them fed, clothed, educated and entertained. Not so much of a problem if you've got a hefty private pension, but a bit of an issue if you're relying on the state.

Young adults are hideously expensive – and it's not just that they eat a lot. Their tastes are dictated by their peer group, and those tastes are about as ephemeral as Scotch mist. Worse – I know quite a few who've jollied off to uni and, without a

Here's an
idea for
you...

**If you've got children over the age of twenty in gainful employment, bully them into starting a pension. Each time one of your children signs up, reward yourself with a slap-up meal. You'll have earned it! One day they'll thank you for this (right now, of course, they'll just resent the interference).**

second thought, blithely announced after the end of year one that they've failed their first-year exams and, anyway, they hate their chosen subject so they're going to start all over again.

Boy, will you resent them. If you're not careful you'll get to the point where you keep a mental tally of the cost of every half-drunk glass of Coke they leave on their bedroom floor. You know I'm right here. It's no good being optimistic about it, you've got to talk to them honestly about your drop in income. If you've always indulged your children it's going to be hard, but remember we don't do our children any favours by teaching them to be extravagant. It's much kinder to explain the realities of life. Explain how much pension you're getting, talk them through how much it's costing to run the house, and come to a sensible compromise on how much allowance they'll get.

Then there's all that free time you've got now. Have a think about whether to put some boundaries around your chauffeuring duties. You can hear the hints already, can't you? Now that you've got all that free time, what's to stop you picking them up at two in the morning? Or, for that matter, why shouldn't they expect you to cook their meals, clean their room and wash their clothes? If you don't want to be taken for granted, best to sort it out now.

## HATING FEELING A BURDEN

Your children might be off your hands and, if you're lucky, they'll be like my daughter: independent, responsible, caring and charming. Yes, I know that sounds smug, but in fact there's a serious downside to this situation

> If you reckon there must be better things to do than worry about your kids, maybe you should get some inspiration from IDEA 31, *Burn the pipe and slippers*

*Try another idea...*

– sooner or later she's going to start worrying about me. Make sure your kids realise you're still the free spirit you always were and that you're intending to have a ball until the far distant day, perhaps, when you reach a point where your children have a genuine right to worry about you. Let them know that you'll appreciate their concern when you're ill and need a hand, but that you'll resent any anxiety over the fact that you're reliving the sixties or swanning about Argentina.

## FED UP WITH BEING ON CALL

This is probably the most difficult one to manage. It's where your ostensibly independent children are secretly hoping to get back to the days when they could always rely on mum and dad to be there for them, night or day. Oh yes, they're off your hands and you're not expected to feed and clothe them but, 'Now you have all this time Dad, it'll be lovely for you to have the grandchildren/decorate our lounge/mow our lawn/clean our house won't it?' Er, yes. Possibly. Or possibly not. The ground rules here are exactly the same as before: make it clear what you are prepared, and not prepared to do. Learn to say a very polite 'no' if you think you're being taken for granted.

> '*The first half of our lives is ruined by our parents, and the second half by our children.*'
> CLARENCE DARROW, American lawyer

*Defining idea...*

*How did it go?*

**Q** **My three children are all asking me to babysit. Frankly there are just too many grandchildren and I'm knackered all the time. But how can I say no?**

*A* *I reckon you need to take control of the situation. Get all your children together and explain that, much as you love your grandchildren, you don't think it's safe, either for them or for you, if you're looking after too many of them at once. Be ready with a list of times when you're prepared to babysit and ask your children to make sure you have no more than one set of grandchildren at any time.*

**Q** **I really struggle communicating with my kids. How can I improve this?**

*A* *Try having an adult conversation with them. Forget for half an hour that they're you're children and pretend they're smart, responsible grown-ups. (Warning for those with delayed families: this won't work with two-year olds, who are just unreasonable by nature!) If possible have a practice run on a fairly non-contentious topic and work out a compromise with them – this way they can get the idea of a win/win solution. Leave it to work for a week or so before you tackle your more important problem, then try the same tactic.*

**Q** **We've always wanted to retire to Italy, but now that the time's come our children are obviously very upset about it. I don't want to hurt them. Should we change our minds?**

*A* *If you're desperate to go, why not get a place that's big enough for your children to come and stay regularly?*

## 31

# Burn the pipe and slippers

**Trust me. You don't want to spend your retirement sitting in an armchair watching TV when you can be having the best time of your life. Work out what gets you really excited.**

You know that old adage that schooldays are the best days of your life? Well I reckon it's a load of nostalgic hogwash.

Whoever coined the phrase had completely forgotten the reality of homework, school dinners and ritual humiliation in the gym class. Now, if the saying went 'Being a kid is the best time of your life', I'd have a bit more sympathy with it, because children's lives should be all about that great mix of values: freedom, fun and a sense of purpose. When you were a child there was no pressure to earn a living, you were encouraged to enjoy yourself and your 'job' was to learn new things. Trouble is, that good balance got lost somewhere in the rat race of adulthood. I've often thought of advertising: 'Lost, somewhere in my thirties, my freedom and half my fun. Reward to finder.'

Now's the chance for us to put that right, and for each of us to say: 'Retirement is the best time of my life.' Freedom's the easy bit – no more alarm clocks, no more packed trains or rush-hour traffic jams, no more rules – but without a bit of

*Here's an idea for you...*

**Write down your key values, one per Post-it note, then divide them into three groups: unimportant; reasonably important; and the ones that make you who you are. Discard the 'unimportant' ones straight away. Recheck the rest, and when you're happy that they are correctly categorised, throw away the 'reasonably important' ones. Choose the three most important of what's left. This will help you decide whether the direction you're planning is the right one.**

planning the fun might elude you, and life without the need to earn a living might feel aimless. Get out the coloured pens and a large piece of paper and start writing down some goals. Start with two simple words: 'fun' and 'purpose', and let your mind run free over the possibilities. What's your idea of fun? What gets your adrenalin going? What would give you a real sense of achievement?

This is exciting! For the first time for years you can learn about stuff that's not relevant to your job, you can take time to do things you've always wanted to try but never had the time, and you can get a real kick out of meeting the kind of challenge you never dreamt you'd have the opportunity to tackle. Forget about those work-related SMART (specific, measurable, attainable, realistic and timely) goals for a minute. Dream a little dream. Is there some skill you'd like to use if you only knew where to start? Some talent you've long neglected? In years to come, when you look back at your retirement, what would you like to have done, who would you like to have met, whose life would you like to have enhanced?

Don't forget to look at some of your long-abandoned hopes. You never know, things that looked impossible thirty years back might now be very achievable. Of course, you may realise that you'd rather die unfulfilled than actually be able to dance like John Travolta in *Saturday Night Fever* (there's a fashion deadline on some ambitions). On the other hand, you might also realise that you could, if you wanted, make Everest base camp since, these days, half the people there seem to be grannies.

**If your freedom is curtailed because you're looking after someone, or if you're not too well and are being looked after by someone else, there are still ways to improve your life. Try IDEA 36, *Who cares?***

*Try another idea...*

If this is going to work, once you've had the nerve to dream your wildest dreams you'll have to turn some of them into real, achievable goals but before you do that spend a bit more time making sure you're really heading off in the right direction. Even seemingly attractive visions, say retiring to sizzle on a Spanish beach and drink endless sangrias, can be traps if it turns out that what drives you most is a taste for adventure, or if you can't bear to leave your country garden. Be brutal about what it is that makes you tick. Don't just concentrate on what's familiar to you.

**'A wise man will make more opportunities than he finds.'**
FRANCIS BACON

*Defining idea...*

**How did it go?**

**Q**   **I do have some goals that I have to achieve, but they don't excite me. What do I do?**

*A*   *We all have goals we can't avoid (clearing the mortgage, losing weight, cleaning the oven) but if you value having a bit of excitement in your life you need more. Look back over your life so far and choose five events that stick in your mind as the best of times. How did you feel? What emotions made the highs so good? Now, think about what kind of experience might help you to recapture those highs. For example, if you got a kick out of learning to drive, you could look for a new skill to learn that would give you that sense of achievement.*

**Q**   **Well, thanks. I tried the 'best of times' exercise and I've just realised that the best fun I had in my life was with people who aren't around any more. Now I feel really depressed.**

*A*   *But you're halfway there! You know your dream needs to include lots of fun and you've realised that you get most fun when you're with other people. All you need to do is find new people.*

# 32

# Try an alternative approach

**Bad back? Try Alexander lessons or an aromatherapy massage. Stressed? What about tai chi or meditation? You're never too old to try alternative therapies, and you may be surprised how effective they can be.**

## Alternative therapies are big news these days.

If you have a medical problem you can choose something that will complement your regular medication; if you're stressed you can choose something to relax you (though they'll all do that to some extent); and if you're fit and healthy you can just choose the one that sounds most fun.

Whatever you go for, there's bound to be somewhere local to you that fits the bill. If you're not sure what's going to suit you (or even what exists) one of the best places to find out about alternative therapies is your neighbourhood health-food store. Even better, if you have a local complementary health clinic it'll have a range of leaflets that explain what's available and what each therapy involves.

Most treatments last about an hour and the cost is usually less than you'd spend on a meal out at your local chain restaurant. They're all pleasant, often fun and there's a million of them, so I'm just going to mention my favourites.

**Treat yourself to an Indian head massage. I can't begin to describe the bliss. You just have to try it for yourself!**

I'll admit that I'm a bit biased when it comes to the Alexander Technique. Invented by a public speaker (named Mr Alexander, oddly enough) who kept losing his voice, it's all about postural alignment. I was driven to try it because of a painful shoulder problem that I'd suffered for years, and I can honestly say that the pain went in a few months. The beauty of the technique is that it's all about doing less, which is a pleasant change in this world where we're constantly exhorted to do more. If you suffer from back pain, or can't get rid of that agonising ache in the neck and shoulders (the feeling that goes along with the tingling fingers and signals a trapped nerve), this is well worth trying. You'll be delighted to know you don't have to wear anything revealing, nor will you be asked to make a fool of yourself.

I'm also a bit biased about aromatherapy massages. It took me a long time to pluck up courage to subject my unbeautiful body to the attentions of a non-medical masseuse, but boy was I converted after the first session. The heady scent of essential oil adds a level of pleasure to a massage that's almost indescribable. Utterly fabulous, and if you haven't tried it you should.

*Defining idea...*

**'For fast acting relief, try slowing down.'**
LILY TOMLIN

How about reflexology? Having your feet massaged is greatly enjoyable even if you remain cynical about the promised benefits. My cynicism disappeared forever when the reflexologist said, after an hour's session: 'Well, I didn't find anything, except for the shoulder of course.' I swear on all I hold dear I hadn't told her. I wasn't in pain that day, so I was moving normally, and she'd neither met me, nor been able to read anything on the booking form that could have given her a clue about my physical state. My daughter's a convert too (for similar reasons), so this one gets a big vote from us.

Read IDEA 44, *Banks don't pay loyalty bonuses*, and find spare cash to pay for the therapy.

*Try another idea...*

If you want to get a little deeper into the alternative lifestyle, daily meditation might sound very Eastern and hippy but it's become almost mainstream these days, and is a great stress reducer with, according to recent research, proven benefits for the heart. Or you can balance your yin and yang in a more active pursuit like tai chi, which must have something going for it because millions of elderly Chinese stand on the streets and wave their arms about every day. I gave up very quickly – I found it intensely irritating to have the teacher move my hand an inch or so because it wasn't perfectly aligned. Not for me, but maybe for you?

*'Man's mind stretched to a new idea never goes back to its original dimensions.'*
OLIVER WENDELL HOLMES

*Defining idea...*

*How did it go?*

**Q** **I know some therapies have been around for donkey's years, but there seem to be some new, and very odd-sounding, ones around. Where's the proof that any of them works?**

A *This is a fair question, because there isn't much research and I have doubts about whether some alternative therapies can possibly provide the benefits they promise. Others (like the Alexander Technique) have a great track record, so you can always do a bit of research before you book a session. Even then, what any alternative therapy provides is an invaluable hour to yourself. If you're tempted to try one of the more avant-garde therapies I suggest you choose one that sounds as if it'll give you some enjoyment and relaxation.*

**Q** **I'm already taking medicine prescribed by my doctor. Should I be going for anything else?**

A *Why not check with your doctor to see if there's any reason you can't help yourself with some alternative therapy to supplement your conventional treatment?*

**Q** **I like the idea of doing something different, but can you suggest anything less, well, passive?**

A *Try a martial art. Stroll along to your local karate club and have a look at what they do with their evening or (my personal recommendation) try aikido. You'll first need to learn to fall because aikido uses a roll rather than the scary back-slapped-on-the-mat approach of most martial arts, but once you've mastered that you'll find it's a fascinating defensive art that uses your opponent's movement against him in the sneakiest way possible. Any martial art will be great fun, a good workout and a really practical way of getting some inner peace and discipline into your life.*

## 33

# Feeling blue?

**Depression is one of the most common illnesses but it's sometimes difficult to spot. So first you have to recognise it; then you have to find enough energy to want to beat it. Learn how.**

With the exception of bottom-of-the-table footie fans (who seem to get more devoted and more gloomy as they age), there's no particular evidence to suggest that older people get more depressed than young people.

In fact there's some evidence that suggests the opposite, which isn't too surprising when you consider how much better it is to be retired than to be on the work treadmill. But older people aren't immune from depression, and things like money worries, bereavement and boredom can cause misery at any age.

I'd better begin by saying that there's a difference between feeling blue and real, clinical depression. We all have that grim Monday morning feeling occasionally – sometimes it even lasts till next Monday. You know the symptoms: there's a

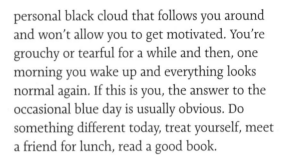

Here's an idea for you... **Smile. When you smile (whether or not it's genuine) your body notes the expression of happiness on your face and assumes you're happy. So then it releases some of those happy hormones which, of course, makes you feel genuinely happy. Just try it out. Yes, now. Go on, smile. The more you smile, the happier you are.**

personal black cloud that follows you around and won't allow you to get motivated. You're grouchy or tearful for a while and then, one morning you wake up and everything looks normal again. If this is you, the answer to the occasional blue day is usually obvious. Do something different today, treat yourself, meet a friend for lunch, read a good book.

Clinical depression is much more difficult to deal with. Despite wishing you could feel better, you don't have the energy to help yourself. In fact, you can reach a point when it's even too much effort to make yourself a cup of coffee.

I won't go into the reasons for depression except to say there can be both psychological and physiological causes, but you ought to be able to recognise the main symptoms so you can spot the beast if it arrives. If you feel 'down' these days, do you also have any of these problems?

- You can't generate interest in anything very much

- Your sleep pattern has become very disturbed recently

- You have no appetite

- You lack energy

- You've had thoughts of suicide

- You're having trouble concentrating

- You're very anxious and tense

- You cry easily

- Your libido has all but disappeared

- You have frequent minor illnesses

- You suffer from lots of minor aches and pains

**If you're depressed because you're not as fit as you were, read IDEA 51, *My arm isn't long enough,* for some thoughts on how to get around your problems.**

*Try another idea...*

*'Make your own recovery the first priority in your life.'*
ROBIN NORWOOD, therapist

*Defining idea...*

145

*'He that won't be counselled can't be helped.'*
BENJAMIN FRANKLIN

If you've ticked more than three of these there's a chance you're suffering from depression. What you really need to do is talk to your doctor (who may begin by checking that there's no obvious cause for the problem, such as hypothyroidism or a reaction to medication).

If you've gone through periods of depression before and are aware that you're not at your best, or if the stress of retirement has made you feel anxious and miserable, learn to stop the downward spiral before it reaches the point where you're genuinely depressed. Watch for early warning signs, such as a change in appetite, loss of libido, increased alcohol consumption, insomnia or poor concentration. Get help.

Treatments for depression include drugs that affect the serotonin level in your body, referral to a counsellor or a psychotherapist (who'll help you work out the reason for your depression and give you some coping strategies) and a bit of self-help. Do as much as you can to help yourself get better. As soon as you feel able, get some exercise, eat healthily and, if there's an opportunity to help someone in need, chip in and remind yourself that you're a lot better off than some people.

**Q**   **There's a long waiting list for a counsellor here. Is there anything else I can do while I'm waiting?**

*How did it go?*

**A**   *Why don't you write down exactly how you feel? Follow this simple format. Paragraph one: write down the facts. What, exactly, has happened to make you feel like this? Paragraph two: describe how you feel. Pour out your emotions. If you feel angry, write it down. If you're sad, let the tears drip from the end of your ballpoint. Get rid of the emotion onto the paper. Leave your writing for a few days and then go back to it. Read it through. Add anything you think you missed, and write down what you've learnt about yourself in the last couple of weeks. Throw the note away. Screw it up; burn it; tear it into little pieces; get rid of the emotion.*

**Q**   **My husband Pete, has got problems at work. I can see he's very depressed and I've tried to talk to him but he refuses to discuss it. It's making me miserable now. How can I make him see the company's counsellor?**

**A**   *You can't. You can suggest that he sees the counsellor but it's up to Pete to decide whether he wants to go. Why don't you go along to the counsellor on your own? Pete might decide to join you and, if he doesn't, you can at least work out how to cope with the situation.*

## 34

# Get into the closet

**Why do so many people dress like old people? What's wrong with being stylish?**

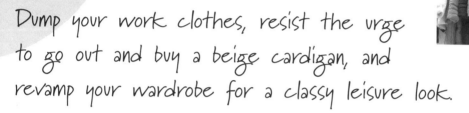

*Dump your work clothes, resist the urge to go out and buy a beige cardigan, and revamp your wardrobe for a classy leisure look.*

Yep, I can see the temptation. You've paid a fortune for the suits, they're still in good nick. Damn it why not recycle them into casual wear?

Or perhaps you're the other extreme? You'd rather walk naked down the high street than dress in the hated work gear again, so you've slung the lot and now have to live in scruffy jeans and the odd posh frock.

Forget all that. Retirement's a new beginning, so you need an entirely new look. Set a bit of cash aside and kit yourself out with a couple of stylish outfits that give you an image that's all your own. Incidentally, that means you mustn't attempt to co-ordinate with your partner or you'll end up looking like Charles and Camilla.

So, what exactly is style? Can pensioners be cool? I think so, as long as we don't break the two cardinal rules.

Here's an idea for you... **Find some large bin-liners. Open your wardrobe. Take out any clothes that you haven't worn for over a year, or that you've no realistic chance (be honest here) of fitting into again, and put these into the bags. Drive straightaway to your nearest charity shop and hand everything over. Leave without looking back. You will feel better, believe me.**

## The mutton and lamb rule

Nothing looks sadder than an old person wearing inappropriate trendy fashions. When I was sixteen I could wear pretty much anything. When I hit thirty I just about got away with platform shoes. Just. If I'd been a few years older I'd have been publicly ridiculed and, as it is, people who see photos of me taken in those days fall about laughing. Follow fashion with care, choosing just one or two classy elements to make you look up to date. (Note I said 'classy'. In my opinion that doesn't include hoodies.)

## The mother-of-the-bride rule

Don't, please don't, dress yourself from head to toe in beautifully co-ordinated clothes like Doris Day in one of those old movies. This applies to men too. Natty blazer, smart slacks, and shoes you can see your face in just scream 'old man'.

## HOW TO CHOOSE

If you feel pretty confident about your ability to buy clothes that make you look good, start working on your new image by doing a bit of pre-shopping research. Buy a child's scrapbook, a stick of glue and half a dozen glossy mags with loads of fashion photos and ads. Choose all the outfits you like best, and stick them in your book. Then work back through your choices to find the common themes. Note what colours appeal to you, what shapes, what materials. At the same time, note what doesn't appeal – have you eliminated everything with a pattern? Are there colours you haven't included?

Then build yourself a capsule wardrobe. Yes, you'll probably have seen this idea before but, if you're like me, you've never been very clear what it means. Well, here's an example of one:

Choose a neutral colour as your base (camel, cream, taupe, brown, black or, sigh, if you must, beige). Let's say you're a woman and you've chosen camel.

**Can't bear to chuck out the old gear? Hoarding's a bad habit – read IDEA 39, *Let's give it up for the wrinklies.***

*Try another idea...*

**'Clothes make the man. Naked people have little or no influence on society.'**
MARK TWAIN

*Defining idea...*

151

**'If people turn to look at you on the street, you are not well dressed.'**
BEAU BRUMMELL

Choose two constrast colours that work well together, and look good against your neutral and one bright accent colour. A capsule wardrobe might begin with:

- a pair of trousers, a skirt, and a smart coat all in camel

- a casual jacket, a pair of trousers and a skirt in one of your contrast colours

- one pair of smart shoes, and one pair of casual shoes in camel

- in each of your contrast colours, two casual shirts or jumpers, and two smart shirts or jumpers

- a couple of accessories in your accent colour – a belt, a scarf, a handbag or another pair of shoes.

That gives you a small, but flexible wardrobe and you can add to it, piece by piece. It's entirely up to you how you put it together, but the key is to make sure you can mix and match every item with every other item.

**Q**   **I've got good quality clothes, though some of them are old, and I don't have much cash. How can I look more stylish?**

*A*   *Get imaginative about what you have. Sometimes we team things up out of habit, and forget we can mix and match. Maybe you have a pair of black trousers that you've always worn with a matching black jacket. Team them with a cream jacket and see how good it looks.*

**Q**   **Fashion changes all the time. How can I stay trendy without breaking the bank?**

*A*   *Never become a fashion victim – keep your basic items of clothing classic and neutral, but keep your eyes open to see what accessories are fashionable. If floppy 80s bows come back yet again (heaven forbid) a cheap blouse is an easy addition to make you look up to date.*

**Q**   **I'm not confident about chosing a look myself. Where can I get help?**

*A*   *If you'd like a bit of help to assemble a new image, one of the great services available these days is the personal stylist. If you're at all unsure about your look you can pay for a half-day session with a stylist, who'll tell you what colours suit you most and what shapes look best on you. If you don't want to fork out the cash, most of the big department stores now offer a personal shopper service. You can sit in comfort in the changing room while a trained member of staff trudges around the floors to bring you what will suit you best.*

How did
it go?

# 35

# Oh. The paint's all dried up

**Take a fresh look at how you spend your leisure time and find some new interests.**

If you've kept unused oil paints in the cupboard for twenty years, ready for the day you have time to use them, you probably were never that keen.

Obviously, the trouble wasn't that I couldn't find the time to get the oil paints out and use them. Because I managed to find time to have a go with the watercolours, time to read loads of books, time to take golf lessons (of which more later) and even time to write 80,000 words of fantasy-fiction novel. No, there was something more to it. To be honest I didn't really know where to start, but it was also possibly just because oils are messy and you need to leave the painting lying about. I didn't fancy living with the smell and I just knew the cat wouldn't be able to resist the temptation to leap on top of the easel and use the painting as a slide. Such a hassle. Finally I gave up and handed them over to Oxfam.

*Here's an idea for you...*

**Give your latest leisure activity more spice by setting yourself a challenge. If you're doing something energetic, like running or swimming, choose a suitable target distance and aim to raise some cash for charity by getting sponsored. If you're learning to jive, enter the first of next year's competitive events. You can't find a challenge? There's always a way of gingering up even a mundane activity.**

Does this sound like you? Do you have boxes of unused beads waiting to be strung? Is there a bag full of hardly used scuba diving equipment stuffed through the loft hatch? Do rows of empty flowerpots await the day you find time to plant tomato seedlings?

If you're not yet retired it's worth hanging on to the equipment, because you just might get around to using some of these expensive toys, but if you've been retired for more than a few months and the cobwebs are still undisturbed, it's time to move on. Flog it all on eBay, or at a boot sale, or give it to charity and find yourself a few new hobbies.

Trouble is, where do you start? It's time for the old pad and pen again, with the page divided up into three columns. Head up column 1, 'Activity', column 2, 'Cost', and column 3, 'Time'. In the first column, write down every leisure pursuit that's ever caught your interest. Spend a couple of weeks adding to the list – pore over your local paper to see what clubs are around; read the Sunday papers to see if anything fascinating crops up in the supplements; talk to friends and family about how they spend their leisure time; check out the TV channels to find a few weird hobbies; stroll around the non-fiction stacks in the library and write down the subject headings. By the time you've finished you should have at least fifty activities on your list, or you're not trying hard enough.

When you've got the magic fifty, you're ready to do some investigation. For each of the activities you should get a rough idea of the cost of any equipment you'd have to buy or hire, what training you'd need before you could begin, and any other costs involved (club membership, travel, etc.). Rule out any that are clearly out of the question because you can't afford them and then move over to column 3.

If you think all this is a bit tame, check out IDEA 2, **Book the bungee jump.**

Try another idea...

This is where you estimate how much time you'd want to give to each new hobby. Sounds obvious I know, but there's not much point in learning to play golf if you've only got a couple of hours a week and your hand–eye co-ordination's as crap as mine (two sets of lessons and I still can't connect the stick-thing with the ball).

'True enjoyment comes from activity of the mind and exercise of the body; the two are ever united.'
ALEXANDER VON HUMBOLDT

Defining idea...

The final stage is to decide which activities are top of your list. Choose a few to have a go at; make them varied, so you have an interesting mix of active, gregarious, solitary and relaxing things to do in your life. A word to the wise – immediately you've made your choices you'll need to take positive steps to begin them. Book lessons, join clubs, buy equipment and get started, or the list will turn into just another box of oil paints, lost in the back of a drawer.

'The real character of a man is found out by his amusements.'
JOSHUA REYNOLDS

Defining idea...

157

*How did it go?*

**Q** **Well, thanks to you I set myself the challenge of completing a local triathlon next year, but maybe I underestimated the prep. My joints are aching and I'm running out of steam well before the finish. I don't want to let my sponsors down but I'm beginning to think I've bitten off more than I can chew. What do I say to them?**

**A** *I expect they'll wait a year if you think you just need more time for training. If you think it's really beyond you, and you don't want to lose face, what about renegotiating with them? For example, if you're running 26 miles you could do a single marathon plus a non-swimming/cycling forfeit of their choice – they'd enjoy that and you'd have a clear conscience*

**Q** **I like the idea of setting myself a challenge, but I don't see how it can work for me. I'm learning to paint in pastels. Where's the challenge in that?**

**A** *I challenge you to get one of your paintings shown at a local amateur exhibition! Or perhaps even better, I challenge you to sell something at the exhibition. There's nothing like having someone hand over hard cash for one of your offerings to boost your artist ego (and motivation).*

# 36

# Who cares?

**One way or another we're all caring for someone, and being cared for in return, but the day may come when this means more than the odd friendly hug, so be prepared.**

Whatever you do, don't jump the gun. The last thing you want to do is condemn yourself to a tiny retirement flat where there's no chandelier to swing from at your ninetieth birthday party.

But if you do reach the point where you need care, or if you become a carer, it's only sensible to make it as easy as possible for yourself. What are the options?

## SHELTERED HOUSING

From the grand old age of fifty you can buy or rent small houses or apartments run by specialist providers for 'old people'. They usually exclude people who can't look after themselves, or can't make private provision to be looked after, but you'll get a feeling of security from a warden – who'll keep an eye on you to make sure you're still alive each morning. (Just kidding.) Mind you, owner-occupied places tend to charge a hefty service charge so make sure you know what you're letting yourself in for.

**Make your home safe and easy to manage because you never know when you'll need a bit of extra comfort. Get plug sockets moved to a height you can reach without stretching. Make sure the lights are bright enough around steps. Put a non-slip mat in the bath and have a grab rail fitted. If all your sofas are soft, squashy and decadent, buy at least one comfortable chair that's easy to get out of.**

## HOME CARE

If you become unable to look after yourself but aren't at the stage where you need permanent care, the obvious option is to stay at home and get some help. Most people do want to stay in their own home, and it's what the government encourages us to do. You may have to wade through a bureaucratic swamp, but you have the right to financial and practical help if you can't look after yourself, or if you're looking after someone who can't manage without you. Services from local authorities and charities include meals on wheels, home helps and transport provision.

The number one problem of staying at home will probably turn out to be the stairs, which mysteriously transform from the wooden hills of Bedfordshire into the north face of the Eiger. Investigate the feasibility of a stair lift. I'm not sure they do them for spiral stairs (but what a ride!) so if your stairs are difficult think about converting a downstairs room into a bedroom. If that's not an option, see if it's possible to have a downstairs toilet installed so at least there's only one trip each day upstairs.

*Defining idea...* *'Time and money spent in helping men do more for themselves is far better than mere giving.'* HENRY FORD

## SOMEONE ELSE'S HOME

Don't rule out the option of living with a family member but do look into all the potential pitfalls before you accept the offer. Obviously a posh granny flat is pretty cool, but if that's not realistic you'll need your own bedroom and a bit of personal space downstairs if you're not going to regret giving up your home.

**There are lots of gadgets available to help you out. IDEA 45, *From Apple to Zimmer*, will point you in the right direction.**

*Try another idea...*

## NURSING HOMES

Aimed at those people who can't manage on their own, these homes will have staff on duty who'll provide basic care, organise meals and, usually, organise therapeutic social activities to keep residents alert. Check very carefully before you choose – go and have a good look around. Is the standard high enough? Are the staff friendly? See if you can arrange a short stay to find out whether the place is suitable.

## CARING FOR SOMEONE ELSE?

Common sense dictates that if you're getting on, so are the people you love, and you may be called upon to do some caring yourself. If that's the case, whatever you do, don't struggle alone. It's tremendously stressful being on call 24/7 so don't feel guilty about asking for help and for organising yourself some time off. At the very least you should be able to get someone in for a couple of hours a week so you can get out and relax, but ideally you should arrange for your dependant to have a week every so often in a nursing home, so you can get a proper break.

*'Money cannot buy health, but I'd settle for a diamond-studded wheelchair.'*
DOROTHY PARKER

*Defining idea...*

161

*How did it go?*

**Q** **I'm pretty fit and healthy but I've seen other people struggle as they get older, so I'd like to make sure my own home stays suitable for me, whatever my needs. Trouble is I don't have much spare cash. Where can I get help or advice?**

*A* *Local authorities have a certain responsibility to help people stay in their own homes – though I doubt you'll get any help until it's absolutely necessary. Still, it's worth checking their website to find out what they can offer in future. When the time comes you might also get some help from charities – check out Age Concern to see what's available.*

**Q** **A stairlift would make a big difference to me, but they are really expensive. Have you got any bright ideas?**

*A* *Many stairlifts are fitted by people who are, shall we say, at the twilight of their lives. It's not surprising, therefore, that there's a healthy second-hand market in slightly used stairlifts. Talk to a local installer and see what you can haggle for.*

**Q** **I have to go into hospital. What's going to happen to my cat?**

*A* *There are a few charities that will provide temporary homes for pets, and some that will take pets permanently if their owners become too ill to look after them. Try a Google search on 'cat sitting' to find lots of ideas.*

# 37

# Planes, trains and free travel passes

**You may be looking forward to the end of commuting, but you'll still have to get around. Review your travel needs, especially if you live somewhere isolated.**

I'm not one of life's eager travellers. If I thought I could retire and just walk to wherever I needed to go I'd be a happy woman. But, realistically, there are places I just can't get to on foot.

So I reckon it's better that I find out what's available than to get a nasty shock the first time I need to use local transport. If you're in the same situation, what do you need to do? Let's look at that local transport angle first. You know your journey to work like the back of your hand, and if you've travelled around in your job you've probably got a good mental picture of the major road and train networks, but do you have any idea what's generally available in your local area? That's where you're

*Here's an idea for you...* **Get a pedometer and don't use the car till you've reached the magic number of 10,000 steps daily (for me it's at least an hour's walking). It's the best exercise you can get, it's environmentally friendly, it'll save you money, and you'll get to know your neighbours. Go for long walks with a friend and enjoy the scenery. If you really love it join a walking club, go rambling or fell walking.**

going to be spending a lot of your time in future. What facilities are within walking or cycling distance? Is there a good local train or rapid transit service? Is there a decent bus service? If so, find out what offers are available. Your local council may well provide concessions on off-peak travel for pensioners.

By the way, talking of buses, if you've not used them for a while don't rule them out. These days they're usually clean, cheap and you can see where you're going. Unfortunately they're, well, they're like, er, buses. You really do seem to wait around for half an hour, only to have three turn up at once.

When you've got a clear picture of your local network, ask yourself whether that's enough, or whether you'll have to use the car to do routine tasks, like shopping and visiting your doctor.

You may be wondering why on earth I'm even hinting that you may be able to do without your beloved car, but there may come a time when you have no choice but to tackle local journeys on foot. This might be because your car's in dock or simply because you're snowed in and need to get a loaf of bread. You might have to visit someone in hospital – and I've yet to find a hospital car park that has spaces available at visiting time. If you can't take the car, can you walk or cycle, or are you going to have to use public transport?

You might be able to forget the car for local trips, but for longer journeys it's not so easy. In the UK you can get a senior railcard if you're over sixty, and an over-fifty card for national coach travel, but these deals are normally tied to off-peak journeys and, of course, they may not take you to the place you really want to be.

**Are you investigating the buses because you're suddenly on your own? IDEA 49, *Life after death*, might be useful.**

Try another idea...

That means you need to include the cost of maintaining your car when you're working out your finances. Include depreciation, insurance, fuel, road tax, servicing and repairs, and don't forget tyres, exhausts and other bits that wear out occasionally. Do you want to renew your car every couple of years, or keep it till it falls apart and then buy another? Either way, you need to make sure you have the funds available and, at the least, you probably need to have a savings account that's specifically kept to one side for the car.

**'Everywhere is walking distance if you have the time.'**
STEVEN WRIGHT, actor and comedian

Defining idea...

*How did it go?*

**Q** **I live in London and have found I can manage without my car for most of the time, but I like to visit each of my sisters for a week each year. One lives in Berkshire and the other's in the Lake District. I hate the train journeys and I always feel sick on coaches. Any ideas how I can get to them both without a car?**

*A* *People often forget just how much a car really costs them to run: we simply trade the money for the convenience without doing the maths. Taking a taxi for medium-length trips a couple of times a year may seem like wild extravagance, but it's cheaper than a year's motoring. For longer trips, why not just hire a car if it's only for a week? Cheap, easy and efficient. If the driving doesn't appeal, why not try looking for a lift? There are websites that link drivers to passengers for journey sharing.*

**Q** **I retired at 65 last year. Am I too old to learn to pass my test?**

*A* *You can certainly pass the test – not so long ago Lord Renton (who was the House of Lords' oldest peer) passed his test at age 94. But if you've never driven before (he'd been driving for years) be warned that the older you are, the more lessons you're likely to need. If you're over 70 you'll have to renew your licence every three years and make a declaration about your fitness.*

# 38

# Balance the health budget

**There's no getting away from it. As we age we are more susceptible to certain illnesses. Still, there are ways of minimising the risks, so let me put you on the right track for a healthy, fit old age.**

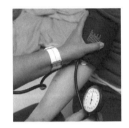

*It's simple. You've heard it all before and there's nothing revolutionary about it.*

Take plenty of exercise; eat healthy foods; eat five portions of fruit and vegetables a day; drink plenty of water; have regular medicals; check yourself for lumps. Blah, blah, blah. Tell me something new, why don't you?

Well, OK. Did you know that you can be ill for years and not realise it? How's this for a list of symptoms that can all be explained away by 'I must be getting old'?

- I sleep very badly, and I'm always tired

- My skin is dry and flaky

- I've got no energy

- I'm moody and I cry a lot

Here's an
idea for
you...

**Measure out two litres of water and put this in the fridge. (Or two bottles of whatever mineral water takes your fancy.) That's what you need to drink a day, as a minimum for good health. If all that water seems just too dull on its own, add some fruit juice to it.**

- God why is it so *cold* in this damned house all the time?

- Why can't I lose weight?

Guessed it? That is, in fact, a list of my own symptoms which, despite showing up in the results from my regular health checks, had gone undiagnosed until an on-the-ball doctor put two and two together and added the sum up to an underactive thyroid.

There are similar lists of 'I must be getting old' symptoms for diabetes, osteoporosis, coronary heart disease, cancer...yes, I know, it's getting worse isn't it? The message is very simple – in fact it's only five words. It hardly warrants a chapter all of its own, except that it needs to be said: **ageing is not a disease.**

Eventually, things don't work as well as they used to, but don't be fooled by that. Lots of people stay fit, healthy and full of energy till the day their bodies finally decide it's time to close up shop. So I'm not suggesting you should turn into a hypochondriac and block-book with your doctor. What I am suggesting is that you keep an eye on your health.

Defining
idea...

*'Effective health care depends on self-care; this fact is currently heralded as if it were a discovery.'*
IVAN ILLICH

## AARGH! WHAT'S THIS?

If a change in your body causes this kind of reaction (or, worse, that ice-cold feeling in the pit of your stomach) don't hang around. Get yourself checked by a doctor. He'll probably reassure you ('No, Mrs Bloggins, it's not a malignant melanoma. You've been creosoting that back fence again, haven't you?'), but if not, at least you've improved your chances of recovery by getting treatment at the earliest possible stage.

## IT'LL EITHER GET BETTER; OR IT'LL GET WORSE

Odd, I know, but I've found it to be a useful little mantra for those annoying little symptoms that don't quite justify seeing a doctor. If something's mildly wrong with you, give it a couple of weeks max. If it's going to get better on its own, it'll have done it by then. If it's not, then it's the waiting-room for you.

For some more thoughts on de-stressing read IDEA 26, *If you think you're stressed now.*

*Try another idea...*

'Hungry Joe collected lists of fatal diseases and arranged them in alphabetical order so that he could put his finger without delay on any one he wanted to worry about.'
JOSEPH HELLER, *Catch-22*

*Defining idea...*

## STOP THE WORLD, I WANT TO GET OFF

If you're always under pressure and never find time to relax you're heading for trouble. At the very least your immune system will be shot to hell and you'll find yourself with one cold after another. Every Sunday morning when you get out of bed, ask yourself 'How stressed am I?' If you feel like a coiled spring, organise some de-stressing action. You might think that retirement will solve all your stress issues, but you'd be surprised. It's never too soon to develop the relaxation habit.

One of the most effective ways to de-stress is to take a spa break. It depends how much you want to spend but there are gazillions to choose from, varying from basic (a back massage and a chicken salad) to posh (five-star retreats in the Swiss Alps with hot stone massages, gourmet food and baths full of bottled fizzy water). Whichever you choose, don't take: work; mobile phone; alcohol; chocolate; loads of clothes –most places supply a towelling robe and, trust me, you won't wear anything else (though there may be a smart/casual rule for dinner). Do take: a couple of novels; smart-but-comfy shoes (you won't want to wear their cardboard flip-flops).

**Q** **I feel awful, with constant pains in my joints. Sometimes I can hardly walk but my doctor says there's nothing wrong. How can I convince him he's wrong and I'm really ill?**

*How did it go?*

A *Log your symptoms carefully for a few weeks and give the list to your doctor (he probably won't thank you). You can, and should, ask for a second opinion if you're really unhappy with the doctor's diagnosis.*

**Q** **I've been to another doctor and had a second opinion. To be fair, the consultant ran a lot of tests, but she agreed with my doctor and had the cheek to say it was all in my mind. I'm at my wits' end. What do I do now?**

A *It is possible that you have a psychosomatic disorder. You could be suffering real, and sometimes considerable, pain for no physical reason. Go back to your doctor and ask if it's worth being referred to a therapist, who can help you explore possible psychological reasons for your pain.*

**Q** **I like the idea of spa break, but it all sounds a bit much. Is there anything simpler?**

A *Try a DIY spa day. Start the day with a workout and a swim, eat light and healthy food, read a novel, forget you even own a phone. Get together the stuff for a home facial. By the end of the day you'll feel less like a corkscrew and you'll look relaxed and in control.*

# 39

# Let's give it up for the wrinklies

**You're still smoking? Alcohol consumption a bit excessive? Break the habit before your doctor starts putting the frighteners on. Try the one-nail-at-a-time approach.**

The trouble with bad habits is that your brain's spent years learning them and now it's automatically geared up to following the neural pathway you've laid down in the grey matter.

For example, one day I realised that every time I walked past the pantry my hand reached in and pulled out the biscuit tin without any conscious instruction from me. It's difficult to give up a habit when you don't even realise you have it half the time.

The trick, then, is to re-educate your brain into laying down new pathways, and there are five basic rules to follow.

**Rule 1:** be clear about the benefits of giving up. You must want to give up; you must want the feeling you'll have when you've given up. Visualise how you'll feel, look and behave when you're free of your unwanted habit. (It's like the old gag:

Here's an idea for you... **Add up the cost of your weekly spend on cigs/booze. Now work out what proportion of your pension income this is. What seemed like an incidental expense when you were earning could now be a financial burden. And healthwise, it's never too late to moderate your habits.**

'How many therapists does it take to change a light bulb? One, but the light bulb has to want to change'.) Then start to behave as though you've already given up – allow yourself to feel like a non-smoker or a slim person. Visualise the new nails, imagine the new harmony when you've stopped nagging yourself. Pretend you've already won the battle. How will you behave differently? How will you feel?

**Rule 2:** identify your triggers. Mine, obviously, was walking past the pantry. If you're a smoker you might automatically light up at certain times of the day, or after meals; if you're a comfort eater you'll be turning to food when you get stressed or miserable; if you bite your nails it might be because you get bored easily.

**Rule 3:** label your triggers. It's all well and good knowing that the pantry door's the trigger for my particular unwanted habit, but if I'm eating biscuits before I even realise it I'm no better off. I have to do something to make that door scream 'no more biscuits' at me. I can, for example, put a padlock on it. If you're a smoker you can set your alarm to go off at the times you know you light up; if you're a comfort eater, stick a 'Don't!' magnet on the fridge or get a notebook and keep a food and mood diary.

Defining idea... *'Only positive consequences encourage good future performances.'*
KENNETH H. BLANCHARD, organisational guru

**Rule 4:** remove temptations. If there are no biscuits in the pantry you can't eat 'em. If there are no cigarettes in the house you can't smoke 'em. You can, of course, stick your coat on and go out to buy some, but that's OK because now we get to...

**Rule 5:** make your lifestyle work in your favour. I'm lazy. If eating biscuits means I have to go to the trouble of getting my shoes, coat and bag and trudging for twenty minutes in the pouring rain to the corner shop, and if there's a half-decent alternative ready in the kitchen, I'll go for the alternative. So I keep dates and nuts on hand and pick at those when the urge for a treat is overwhelming. If you're a smoker, the obvious solution is to have nicotine gum or patches ready to take the yearning away. Have some strategies ready for times when the temptation's overwhelming – take a walk, run a bath, write a chapter of your novel.

If you can't believe you can give up a habit you've had for half your lifetime, read IDEA 42, *Look back in anticipation*: it might help you work out what exactly you're getting out of it.

*Try another idea...*

There is a point, though, when habit breaking needs more than a few rules. Some habits aren't really habits, they're addictions. Smoking comes into that category, but enough people give it up to prove that it can be done without professional help (though don't hesitate to get it if you need it). If you have a drug habit, or if you're secretly worried about your alcohol consumption – or if your nearest and dearest are worried – you need professional help now. You've reached an age where you need every ounce of extra edge you can get to keep healthy and fit so don't kid yourself any longer: be willing to use any resource you can get to help you kick the addiction.

*'I tried to stop smoking cigarettes by telling myself I just didn't want to smoke, but I didn't believe myself.'*
BARBARA KELLY

*Defining idea...*

**Q** **I've tried to end my nail-biting habit but I simply relapse. Have you any suggestions?**

*A* *Go for the one-nail-at-a-time approach. It's about as simple as it gets. It's based, of course, on a nail-biting habit, but with a bit of imagination you can adapt the method for almost any bad habit. For the next month, on no account bite the thumbnail on your right hand. Paint on vile tasting stuff; wear a thumb stall; stick an alarm bell on it if it helps. Just don't bite it. Do a month then raise the stakes to two nails. Keep that up until you've got two beautiful nails and aren't even tempted to bite. Just keep adding fingers.*

**Q** **OK. It worked well and I've got nine beautiful nails. I just can't leave the last one alone! How can I go that last step?**

*A* *How frustrating for you! What about substituting a less self-destructive habit. Wear a ring on that finger and twist it, take it off, fiddle with it every time you find yourself biting the nail.*

**Q** **How does the one-at-a-time approach work for other habits?**

*A* *It's far easier to make one small change, then another...and another, than to go cold turkey!*

## 40

# 'I used to be someone, but now I'm retired'

**If you thought it was bad telling people you were a dentist/right-wing despot/tax inspector, it's worse telling them you're retired. Find a way to describe yourself that will give you real status and won't trigger that glazed look of boredom in new acquaintances.**

## As an occupation, 'retirement' doesn't sound too important does it?

Despite years of trying, nobody has managed to come up with an alternative word that sounds sexy and makes people wish they, too, had that wonderful status. 'Pensioner' is depressing, 'a member of the third age' is, frankly, ridiculous and I'm not going to embarrass you or myself with some of the more trendy euphemisms I've heard.

The trouble is that we're often prouder of our jobs than we are of ourselves. I don't know about you, but I can't remember a single instance where someone has answered the question 'What do you do?' with 'I spend my time being a warm-hearted person with a great sense of humour' (or even 'I'm training to be a vicious bully with a nasty temper', which is surprising because I've met a few of those).

*Here's an idea for you...* **Try using a bit of coaching on yourself. You don't think you have any expertise? Write down everything you've ever done and been proud of; everything you've ever enjoyed. It doesn't have to be anything highly skilled; nor does it have to be seriously intellectual. (For example, if you've brought up four kids and they're all doing OK, you're an expert at child rearing.)**

Could you give that kind of answer? Think about it for a minute. If someone said that to you, wouldn't you be just a bit interested? Wouldn't you want to know more?

A bit too radical for you? Prefer to talk about your hobby? Well, if you've just had a painting hung in the local gallery, why not say so? If you have a life full of fun, excitement and challenge, don't tell people 'Oh, I'm retired now but I used to be a chicken-plucker.' Make them jealous – give them a huge grin and say 'Oh, I'm having a great time. I spent yesterday _____ have you tried it? Anything interesting will fill the gap – sky-diving would be good perhaps?

Mind you, just as 'tax inspector' probably gets your new acquaintance frantically looking for an escape route, there's a right and a wrong way of talking about your interests. A guy I met at a friend's wedding lectured me on golf techniques – I swear he didn't draw breath for an hour. He clearly missed the status his old job had given him and to compensate he had turned to pontificating about his hobby to make him feel important. The silly thing was that I'd have loved some coaching from an expert. Despite a shed-load of lessons I'm still at the stage where I get excited if I actually manage to hit the ball.

*Defining idea...* **'The worst of work nowadays is what happens to people when they cease to work.'**
G. K. CHESTERTON

If he'd asked me whether I played, and whether I was any good, I'd have happily demonstrated what I loosely call my 'swing' and accepted some impromptu help.

Fancy getting back with old friends now you've got a new identify? Find out how with IDEA 43, *Who loves ya?*

*Try another idea...*

You don't have to bore people. Instead, whatever your particular field of expertise, you can make it work for you by using simple coaching techniques. Don't fall into the trap of telling people how to do things. Instead, assume that everyone has the capacity to overcome their difficulties and use your knowledge to help them to find the answers within themselves. Get them to outline their problem (or demonstrate their swing!) Probe a little to make sure you understand – and more importantly that they understand what's wrong. Ask them what options they have, and guide them towards their own way of managing their problems.

So, if you've asked yourself 'Is there a purpose to my life after retirement?' and you've answered 'No', think again. Tell yourself instead: 'I'm finally free to choose my reason for living.' To coin a phrase – this isn't the beginning of the end; it's the end of the beginning.

'Advice is seldom welcome, and those who need it the most, like it the least.'
LORD CHESTERFIELD, 18th century politician

*Defining idea...*

*How did it go?*

**Q   Friends often come to me for advice, but they never seem to take it. What am I doing wrong?**

A   *It may sound odd, but people don't really want advice, even if they ask for it – and they'll never take it if it isn't what they want to hear. (Deep down, of course, we all know the answers to our problems. It's just that sometimes we can't face those answers.) So remember that people have to reach their own decisions. What they'll value from you is help in surfacing and clarifying their options. Question, summarise and challenge, then be silent. People don't like silence, so it's a very effective technique for making them talk. Under pressure like that they often dig deep and find the solution they're looking for.*

**Q   I'd like to make some real use of my life experience. Any ideas?**

A   *Become a guru. You think anyone ever asks Mandela, 'What do you do?' Of course, it helps that he's mega-famous, but more than that he's respected for his experience and people accept that he's still got plenty to offer. You can be the same. Being a guru (OK, 'consultant' if you prefer) isn't necessarily about trying to launch a second career. It's about believing in yourself, and making others believe your knowledge and opinions still count. Go away right now and think about something you do really well, and how you would brand yourself as a consultant. (You could even get some business cards printed.)*

# 41

# Get an MOT

**No, silly. Not the car – you. Regular health checks really are worthwhile, believe me.**

If you had the choice, would you go for a long gradual decline into illness and infirmity, or would you prefer to stay fit and healthy for a few decades yet, till the day your heart decides it's had enough?

It's a bit of a no-brainer isn't it? People do tend to worry about becoming ill or infirm as they age but we're a healthy generation with lots of medical backup, and most of us will stay fit for a long time to come if we're sensible.

Being sensible includes taking proper measures to prevent disease, and one of those measures can be to have regular health checks. These can be pretty nerve wracking. Despite evidence to the contrary I always have an upset stomach the day of a medical because I'm convinced I'm going to be diagnosed with something gruesome. Take some of the stress out by staying as fit as you can – keep your weight in the normal range to reduce the chance of being told you've an obesity-related illness like Type 2 diabetes or heart disease, and exercise regularly to keep your body strong and your heart fit.

**Check your blood pressure. This can increase without causing you any symptoms, but racking up a lot of future health problems. If you don't want to bother your doctor with this (and many people find surgeries so stressful that their blood pressure increases anyway), there are now some neat DIY devices you can buy.**

If you're still at the stage of planning your retirement and your employer provides health screening it's obviously sensible to pop along before you leave. I know there's been some controversy about these checks – mostly because the people who get them are the people who look after themselves anyway, partly because they get people worried about things that can be safely ignored but, hey, many of the major illnesses associated with age are preventable. Many are curable if found early. If a routine test can find cancer well before I'd notice any symptoms or if it can tell me my heart's not working at its optimum before I realise I'm more out of breath than my peers – I reckon it's worth having done.

Depending on which provider you choose, a private health screening could include checks on your heart, your lungs, your blood and urine and a physical examination – at one fell swoop you get checked for a whole range of potential medical problems, like liver disease or anaemia.

If you don't have cover, or if you're already retired, it's possible to get some of the same checks on the National Health Service but you'll need to ask your doctor what's available, because provision varies from one area to another. Your doctor won't have any objection to checking your blood pressure occasionally (in fact she probably won't give you much choice about having it checked if

*'I don't want to achieve immortality through my work...I want to achieve it by not dying!'*
WOODY ALLEN

my doctor's anything to go by) and she'll probably have a routine well-man/well-woman clinic that will carry out some of the standard tests for you.

**If the idea of an MOT scares the hell out of you, maybe you're just over-anxious. Read IDEA 46, *Be needed, not needy*, for some help.**

*Try another idea...*

Incidentally ladies, if you're used to having a prompt to go for a regular mammogram be warned that, oddly, there are some age restrictions so you may reach a stage when you're not offered one. No, there's no logic that I can see, just sheer age discrimination.

Another possibility is to pay one of the private health schemes for an annual check up. Even if you don't have insurance you'll find that you can pay for a full health screening – though you won't find it a cheap option!

Don't forget to include visits to your dentist and optician in your programme because both are important monitors of some diseases – like oral cancer or glaucoma.

Finally, a couple of small hints. Gentlemen, if you can't get a good night's sleep because of the constant need to pee, see your doctor and get your prostate checked. And, while we're on the subject, ladies, if you suffer from stress incontinence (coughing, laughing or some sudden movement are the usual triggers) you, too, need to talk to your doctor, because this condition is treatable.

*'He decided to live forever or die in the attempt.'*
JOSEPH HELLER

*Defining idea...*

*How did it go?*

**Q** **I hear what you say, but I haven't had a medical since I was in my thirties and I'm scared stiff of what they might find. Am I being stupid?**

*A* *No. Everyone feels like that, but the majority of people are fine and it's a very reassuring process. In fact, if you get a clean bill of health you feel wonderful. However, if it turns out that there is something wrong, you just have to remember that the problems we're talking about don't improve with neglect, so not knowing you have warning signals is always going to be worse than finding out you've got some early symptoms and getting treatment.*

**Q** **But I feel perfectly OK so why do I need to bother?**

*A* *Some conditions (e.g. furred arteries) don't show up until they're well advanced and harder to manage. I reckon it's better to have an early warning. But it's up to you!*

**Q** **Is it worth checking myself over, or should I just leave this to the pros?**

*A* *It's a good idea to look at your body each month to see if you have any new lumps or swellings. Remember to check your skin for any moles that seem to have changed shape or colour. Most women are taught to carry out regular breast checks and the need for these doesn't diminish when you retire. If you're not sure how to do this, ask your doctor to show you. Men need to be vigilant too – for example testicular cancer is much easier to deal with in its early stages, so check yourself regularly for unusual lumps or swellings, or any painfulness.*

# 42

# Look back in anticipation

**How's it working for you so far? Is retirement everything you hoped for, or did you try a few things and then get stuck in an uncomfortable comfort zone? Why not call 'time out' to make a progress check?**

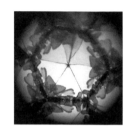

I'm a bit embarrassed to admit that I'm the kind of person who prefers to read the last page first.

I'm always in a hurry to get to where I'm going, or to see a conclusion to what I'm doing and I have to force myself to slow down, reflect and take one step at a time. If you're like this, give yourself a break and spend ten minutes now reflecting on how your retirement is panning out.

If everything's great, well done. If not…perhaps you've concluded that you're busy but you've got a bit bored with the same old same old? Perhaps you've decided nothing's turned out right and you're miserable? Or maybe you've realised you're so busy that your head feels like one of those kaleidoscope toys you had as a kid – full of whirling bits of colour that keep falling into enticing patterns but never actually settle on one for long enough for you to enjoy it?

*Here's an idea for you...*

**Keep a reflection diary. Every time something makes you feel lousy write a note of what exactly happened. Be as objective as possible, just recording the bare facts. Then describe how you felt, and how you behaved. You can be as descriptive or as terse as you like. Try to look calmly and objectively at the event. How did you react to events? How could you have acted differently? How could you act if it happened again?**

If any of these sounds like you, you need to find more time to think. Choose a quiet place where you can be alone for half a day, boot up the laptop, or get a pencil and paper to scribble down ideas, put the kettle on and put your feet up.

Look back closely over the last year. Did you do any of the things you'd planned for your retirement? Remember those day-one goals and work out where you are with each of them.

Maybe you've achieved them all – in which case you probably didn't set the bar high enough, and you need to get some new goals.

Or perhaps you got lost in a morass of routine activities? That may mean you have to take some serious action to make time for the things you really want to do.

Perhaps you set the bar too high? If you've given up on your goals because you can't make any progress towards them, have a think about whether they're impossible dreams, or whether you still think you can achieve them. If you're still keen to have a go, break each goal into tiny steps, and get ready to work through them methodically. There's something about this kind of plan – it's a bit like crossing a rickety bridge. You gingerly step from one plank to another, feeling as though it's taking for ever, then you look back and find, wow, you're two-thirds of the way across and it's easier to go forward than back.

Possibly something came along that threw all of your plans out of the window and you're feeling unhappy and put-upon? Maybe you need to revisit your goals to set some that are more achievable in your changed circumstances?

Now, narrow down your review, and concentrate on the past month. What have you done? What did you enjoy? What did you loathe? Where were the boring bits? How many new experiences did you have? How do you feel today?

Make some long-term plans, but if things aren't going so well, don't try to fix everything at once. Choose a couple of small things that you can change without too much trouble so you can feel some immediate improvement in your life; then choose a couple more. Bit by bit you'll find life begins to look better.

**Can't find time for reflection? Improve your time-management skills with IDEA 52, *First amongst equals.***

*Try another idea...*

*'To look backward for a while is to refresh the eye, to restore it, and to render it the more fit for its prime function of looking forward.'*
MARGARET FAIRLESS BARBAR, writer

*Defining idea...*

187

How did it go?

**Q** **I don't have time to reflect. Is it really worth the effort?**

*A* *Yes, I think it is, particularly if you keep the diary for a few weeks, because you then begin to see patterns in the way you deal with situations. I was forced to keep a diary like this for a course I took, and I was amazed at how much I learnt when I worked back through it for my end-of-term assignment. It's a good way of learning how to do things better.*

**Q** **I have a very difficult neighbour and I've found that keeping a reflection diary helps me a lot – I seem to be able to get rid of a lot of my anger just by writing about what happened and how I felt. The only problem is that it doesn't help me deal with the pest next door. Is there anything else I can try?**

*A* *Recording the facts and the emotions is, as you say, a good way of venting your feelings, but it won't help you find a way through the problem unless you follow through to the final stage and think about how else you could have handled the situation. For example, if you got angry and shouted at your neighbour, reflect on how things might have gone if you'd calmly agreed that you could see his point of view and proposed a compromise.*

# 43

# Who loves ya?

**You're probably beginning to realise that life's too short to fall out with people you love. Is it too late to put things right? Of course not. It just takes a bit of know-how (and some courage).**

I suppose it's inevitable that you start thinking about the past when you're going through the process of retirement, and it's a time when some real regrets can start to nag at you.

Squabbles, particularly family squabbles, can get out of hand very quickly, and when you look back over the space of many years you can suddenly realise how trivial the whole thing was. Did it really matter that she had the pearls and you only got the garnet? Was what he said genuinely unforgivable? Are you suddenly wondering whether, through all the years of bitterness, you've got it all wrong? Do you miss her?

Sometimes you have to accept that a relationship is over. If your childhood sweetheart has left you after thirty years, moved to the other side of the world and not left a forwarding address, take the hint. If your son's cut off all contact and

**If you've drawn a blank in your search for long-lost relative, try the Salvation Army. They are extremely efficient at locating missing people.**

you've tried and failed to reach him so many times that you can't bear to try again, why reopen the wound? But if you really do want to put things right with some long-lost loved one, even if you've tried before and been rejected, perhaps it's worth one last attempt?

If you'd like to try but you're wondering whether it's worth the risk of being rejected, the best test is to examine the depth of your feelings. If you still feel mild irritation that your nephew backed his car into your front porch, or if you grit your teeth with exasperation every time you remember how your brother-in-law always got your name wrong, it rather suggests that you don't have much invested in the relationship – so you won't feel desperately hurt if your attempts at rekindling it don't work out.

But if you can't bear to touch the wound, and your stomach churns every time you think of your brother's name, it obviously goes much deeper. If you feel this is a nagging pain that's going to take the edge off your great retirement plans you have two options.

**Defining idea...**

*'How much more grievous are the consequences of anger than the causes of it.'*
MARCUS AURELIUS

You could bring the issue to the surface, perhaps by discussing it with a good friend or a counsellor, and try to find a way to work through the emotion and get it in a better perspective. This may well be the right course of action in some cases – if you were abused by a family member, why would you want to establish friendly relations again? Much better to come to terms with the issues, acknowledge your feelings and then put them behind you.

Your other option is to make contact – which means you've decided it's worth taking the risk of getting hurt. Making contact doesn't mean you have to grovel (despite the fact that you still think you were in the right). Neither does it mean you have to make the other person put things right. You can change your own behaviour but you can't make someone else change theirs.

If the person you're feuding with is your partner, read IDEA 4, *Just get out from under my feet, will you?*

*Try another idea...*

The key, therefore, is to act differently. Relegate the past to its proper place, forget about it, and begin the relationship again with kindness. If you're successful and you re-establish relationships, never *ever* refer to the quarrel.

Of course, if you've lost touch entirely with someone but would love to see them again you might have a bit of trouble finding them. Start by writing to their old address or phoning their old number. You might just get lucky and speak to them direct, or to someone who knows where they are now – they might even still have their post redirected. Try family members who could still have a contact address. But if the obvious sources don't work there are various ways of locating missing friends. The Friends Reunited website is an excellent resource for contacting old school-friends; the electoral roll is an interesting way of finding people again; telephone directories world-wide are now searchable via the internet.

*'Who dares nothing, need hope for nothing.'*
JOHANN VON SCHILLER

*Defining idea...*

**How did it go?**

**Q** **What's the best way of making a first contact with my estranged brother?**

**A** *One of the best ways of re-establishing friendly relations with a long-lost friend or relative (especially if there was a falling-out) is to write a letter, because it doesn't put the receiver under any pressure. The letter needs to be short, simple and friendly, and if there was a row you shouldn't talk about forgiveness (which just says 'I was right and you were wrong'). Instead you should say that you regret that you're no longer in touch and would like to put the past behind and be friends again.*

**Q** **I wrote to my daughter and the letter came back 'return to sender'. I phoned and she hung up. What next?**

**A** *This is very sad, but if she's determined not to speak you may have to accept her decision. However, you could try getting a third party to mediate for you. If the mediation fails, give up gracefully, but ask your mediator to make it clear that you are always willing to become part of your daughter's life again if she changes her mind.*

**Q** **My brother has written to me after twenty years of silence. I don't really want to know. What should I do?**

**A** *You may one day regret closing the door, so how about a compromise? Write back in pleasant terms, thanking him for getting in touch and saying you're well and happy, but that you don't feel you want to meet at the moment.*

## 44

# Banks don't pay loyalty bonuses

**There are better ways to manage your investments than playing safe with the old deposit account. Make your savings earn more with a bit of research and some nifty footwork.**

*My motto is, 'I want it now.'*

Years of careful research have taught me that my real talent with money lies in spending it, rather than saving it, and I couldn't care less whether I'm getting a bargain as long as I can take my new purchase with me. (Shopkeepers be warned, I'll only wait for things to be delivered if there's clearly no way my husband can stuff them in the back of the car – why else do you think we bought a hatchback?)

As a result of this cavalier attitude to cash my money's never worked very hard for me, but impending retirement has had a dramatic effect. I'm still struggling with the spending habits, but I've at least done my homework about savings, and I've found that, despite the vast array of financial products, the choice boils down into three varieties.

Here's an idea for you...
**If you haven't got one already, think about opening a internet-based savings account. They usually offer very competitive rates of interest, and as it's so easy to move money in and out, you're more likely to take advantage of this.**

## INSTANT ACCESS CASH

This is the cash we need for everyday spending and routine bills. It won't earn anything for you, because banks and building societies generally don't pay enough interest to cover inflation on this type of account. Nevertheless, there are differences between banks, so if you've had the same account for a number of years it will pay you to check what else is on offer. You may, for example, be able to get a slightly higher rate of interest on an account that's used as a 'feeder' for a low-interest current account.

Obviously, if you allocate too little to this account you'll end up paying the bank for an overdraft; if you allocate too much the bank will be paying you virtually nothing for the use of your cash. Either way, like bookies, the bank always ends up winning so this pot of money needs to be watched very carefully.

## DELAYED ACCESS SAVINGS

This is what we set aside for special purchases, like holidays or presents, or boring things like fridges. So this money needs to be reasonably easy to get at, but we can do a bit of planning and we don't need instant access. The easiest option is to find the fixed interest rate account that's currently paying the most (and check regularly, because banks have a sneaky habit of quietly introducing better accounts to attract new customers). You may have to give three months' notice that you want your cash – although you can always draw instantly if you're prepared to lose some of your interest.

Ideally, you should top this up regularly from income – some accounts pay higher interest if you save regularly into them. If you're on a low income you may need to top it up with cash from your longer-term savings. How much goes into it? Well, that depends on your preferences. If, like me, you like the goodies, you might not want to put a year's spending into it (I'd just spend the lot in the first three months – then I'd either top it up from long-term savings or grouch for the rest of the year).

**In the mood to tackle your finances once and for all? Read IDEA 5, *Spend it like Beckham?***

*Try another idea...*

'**It is sheer madness to live in want in order to be wealthy when you die.**'
JUVENAL

*Defining idea...*

195

Defining idea...

*'The highest use of capital is not to make more money, but to make money do more for the betterment of life.'*
HENRY FORD

## LONG-TERM INVESTMENTS

Lots of people just don't have any money in this category but if you're lucky enough to have a crock of gold to lock away for a long time there's a catch: it gets complicated. Where, amongst all of the options available to you, do you stash it? And no, under the mattress is not an option (especially not for crocks).

Think risk. Are you a gambler or do you need to play safe? If you don't have much cash to play with, or if you only ever play safe, look at things like ISAs, National Savings and Investments, and gilts, but be warned that along with low risk comes a low return.

If you like a bit of a gamble you *must* spread your risks. Think about unit trusts, investment trusts, equities and corporate bonds, but don't invest without doing the research. Don't touch derivatives unless you really know what you're talking about! Why? Well, remember that James Bond scene when the sharks were circling....

**Q** **I get a bit bored with thinking about savings. Is there any way to spice it up a little?**

*How did it go?*

**A** *How about starting an investment club with friends? Each of you puts in a sum of money (which can be as much, or as little as you like) and you invest the pool on the stock market. You'll need to have a written – and signed – contract between you (so you won't fight over the winnings), and you'll have to become very knowledgeable about market movements but you could have some fun and, if you turn out to be a canny investor, you could be drinking champagne for breakfast every morning.*

**Q** **I own my own house but I've got no savings, very little pension and I'm desperate to get a bit more cash. Any ideas?**

**A** *Could you take in a lodger? Sell off some of your garden? Move to a smaller, cheaper property? As a last resort you could opt for an equity release (a kind of re-mortgage) but please take proper financial advice first, because the terms of these deals vary widely and you could be storing up trouble for the future.*

**Q** **You don't mention buy-to-let. Don't you think it's a good idea?**

**A** *There's always a risk that the property market will fall, or that the rental market will dry up. Don't buy-to-let if it ties up all your capital.*

# 45

# From Apple to Zimmer

**Life used to be grim – imagine being old in the fourteenth century. Then celebrate your luck by taking advantage of the great resources available today. From computers to walking aids there's almost certainly something out there to make your life better.**

*Wouldn't it be nice to have loadsamoney when you retire? Hmm. I wonder how many of us are in that position?*

I guess most retired people are on an income that's way lower than they've been used to and, if they're lucky, they may have a bit of rainy day cash in the bank. It's very irritating: now we've got the time to play, most of us can't afford the toys!

If your retirement income stretches to buying a new Ferrari with built-in massage seats I'm delighted for you. (Well, no, that's a total lie. In fact my only emotion is jealousy.) But if you're on a budget, and have to be a bit more discriminating about what you buy, how do you decide which gadgets, from the vast range available, are the ones that'll improve your life the most?

**Check out organisations that exist for 'old' people: they often give great deals on products and services. Lots of these will be local, and an internet search will pay dividends. Don't just do a global search – make your search specific on both 'age' and the name of your home town. You'll get a huge list – but you'll have to plough through a fair bit of dross to get to the few really useful sites.**

Don't reach for one of those catalogues that has all the things you never knew you needed. You know the kind I mean – they all sell that giant furry slipper thing that you can put both feet in. How does that work then? Do you have to bunny hop around the house? What's the point? No – avoid this approach to buying at all costs, because these catalogues are compulsive, and before you can turn around you'll have a house full of cucumber twirlers and Simpsons bottle openers. You haven't seen a Simpsons bottle opener? Well, it glugs, gurgles, fizzes and Homer yells 'beer' very loudly several times. My husband loves the bloody thing.

Ask yourself instead, what do you struggle with? What drives you mad? If you can identify your worst problems you're nearly halfway there. Now, all you have to do is find out whether there's some nifty gadget that can make your life better.

Defining idea... **'We must make the best of those ills which cannot be avoided.'**
ALEXANDER HAMILTON

Some things are easy and obvious, because we all know about them. If you can't bear raking the leaves off the lawn, get a garden vac (or a gardener); if you can't open cans, get an electric can opener; if you can't make the stairs, get a stairlift. Other things need a bit of research. For instance, has anyone invented a sensor that'll lock the catflap every time my revolting pet tries to bring in another field mouse for me to play with? How do you stop the washing machine eating one sock per cycle? Try looking in:

**Revamping your home is a great excuse to buy some gadgets. Work through IDEA 17, *Get the pasting table out of the attic.***

*Try another idea...*

- *Your local library.* If they don't have the helpful book you think must exist, for a small fee you can get most books on an inter-library loan

- *Your local authority.* They have certain obligations to help pensioners and they often have unexpected sources of aid

- *Charities.* Don't feel embarrassed about this. Charity shops are an obvious source of the weird and wonderful, but charities themselves exist for a purpose, and if it's remotely close to what you want they'll be glad to advise

- *Support groups.* If your problem's caused by an illness, it's a pound to a penny there'll be a support group (or more than one)

- *Specialist retailers.* The old walking fingers will find out what's out there for you

- *Hospitals.* If you've been injured, or you are suffering from an illness that requires hospital visits, ask the hospital whether they supply any aids.

'*My grandmother is over eighty and still doesn't need glasses. Drinks right out of the bottle.*'
HENRY YOUNGMANN, actor

*Defining idea...*

How did it go?

**Q** **I've always used a computer at work and I bought myself a laptop before I retired. I'm used to the firm's backup, so I don't know anything about virus checking and I'm really worried about logging on to the internet. Where do I begin?**

*A* *The software provided with your computer will get you started, and there are lots of magazines that'll give you advice. Oddly enough, the best way of getting protected is to download software from the web, but of course you have to take the plunge and log in first. Have you got a grandchild who could help you get set up? They might be happy to be asked.*

**Q** **I live in the country, and my biggest problem is the spiders that seem to roam freely around my home. I loathe them and, though I try to catch them with a glass (you know, you drop the glass over the spider and then push a card under the glass) they always seem to get squashed between the card and the glass. Help!**

*A* *Easy. You need a spider catcher. They're a kind of glass-and-card combination (only in plastic) and have the huge bonus of being stuck on the end of a long plastic stick, so you don't actually have to get close to the monsters. Most gadget mags have them.*

## 46

# Be needed, not needy

**It's horribly easy to lose your independence. It usually starts when you start relying on other people to do things you can do yourself. Take responsibility for yourself. Even better, take responsibility for someone else.**

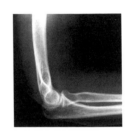

*We take our independence for granted, but perhaps we need to actively nurture it.*

Ever had a broken arm? Remember when they took the plaster off? Some guy walked in with a chain saw and proceeded to hack through the plaster towards your delicate body. When the plaster fell away you immediately stretched out your arm, partly as a kind of high five – sheer relief at the escape from amputation – partly for the hell of it after being trapped in a cast for so long, and partly to ward off further maniac attempts at your anatomy by the guy in the white coat. And the result? Agony. The pain in your arm was far worse than the original break. In six weeks flat your muscles had shrunk into non-existence and it took three months of brutal physio to get back to normal.

In other words, the slide into helplessness is insidious. It's much easier, and faster to lose the ability to do something than it is to get it back. Muscle atrophy is bad enough, but even worse than that is the situation where you've lost your confidence. One day you're hesitating about whether you can face the drive up to your holiday home, the next you're reluctant to get the car off the drive at all.

**If you lack confidence, commit yourself to some kind of group action. Choose your activity, pay in advance, get it in your diary, and arrange to meet someone there. If you've retreated into your shell, pick up the phone and book up for a series of classes in something you've never tried before – local colleges run everything from am-dram to woodwork.**

The best way to deal with this problem is not to let it get you in the first place. Whatever you're doing, keep doing it. Do it more, and try to do it better each time. That way you don't lose either the ability or the confidence and there's no need to read the rest of this chapter.

If you're already feeling dependent and anxious read on.

There are two types of dependence. The first is an emergency state, and it's not easy to get around this one. If you're so ill with flu you can't even get out of bed to get yourself a drink of water, you're just going to have to accept that you need someone to help you today.

The other type of dependence is long-term, and it can vary from an extreme condition (e.g. severe stroke victims) down to an infuriating pseudo-dependency that drives everyone else mad.

*'Make yourself necessary to somebody.'*
RALPH WALDO EMERSON

At the 'extreme' end – well we'd all expect someone with a serious physical or mental disability to be heavily dependent, but even these people should be encouraged to be independent to some extent – and they'll usually want that. If we do everything for our dependants we risk robbing them of their self-respect. If you're helpless, even being able to lift a drink for yourself can be hugely satisfying. My 95-year-old mother-in-law was obviously delighted to tell me the other day that she'd polished a cupboard 'because the cleaner never does it properly'.

Then at the other end of the scale are the tragic people who aren't really dependent at all – they've just lost their confidence. If this is you, try this exercise:

If you're not very independent and you're nervous, read IDEA 11, *Safety first?*, for some ideas about how to feel more confident.

*Try another idea…*

Ask yourself: What's the thing that's scaring me? Why am I so scared?

Imagine yourself doing the thing you're too scared to attempt.

What's the worst that could happen? How would you feel if it did?

If it happened, how could you deal with it? Think this one through in detail, right down to ambulances if necessary.

How likely is it that the worst will happen?

How can you minimise the risks?

Take steps to minimise the risks and to ensure you can deal with the worst.

Do it. You'll be anxious, but keep telling yourself that 'it's only anxiety. It won't hurt me'.

When you've done it, you'll probably be so elated that you'll want to do it again quite soon – and you won't be anywhere near as anxious next time.

**'For they conquer who believe they can.'**
JOHN DRYDEN

*Defining idea…*

205

How did
it go?

**Q**   **It's all right for you to preach on about being independent. After years slaving over a keyboard, I have RSI and need a lot of help. What am I supposed to do?**

*A*   *You may not feel you're actually 'disabled', but it's worth looking in one of the specialist shops because there are lots of aids around to help you get a bit more independence.*

**Q**   **Everything you've said rings loud bells, but unfortunately the dependant isn't me, it's my wife, so I can't really see what I can do about it. Any ideas on making someone else more independent?**

*A*   *Sometimes you have to be cruel to be kind. Before you do that though, make sure you're not over-estimating what your wife is able to do – because you don't want to be just plain cruel. However, if you genuinely know that she could do more for herself, why not talk to her (kindly but assertively) and explain that you're concerned she's over-reliant on you. Tell her that you're worried in case something happens to you and she can't do even simple things for herself. Get her to be more independent in some very small area, and with luck it will grow from there.*

# 47

# Location, location, location

**A place in the country sounds great. But wait – you need shops, pubs, restaurants! And where's the local doctor's surgery, or the dentist? Before you downsize, give some thought to local facilities.**

What looks like an idyllic retreat may turn out to be a rural prison.

I'm not being ageist or rude here. I'm not assuming that anyone over retirement age automatically needs a doctor within walking distance, nor am I expecting you to spend your retirement in the pub. You might even want to have some things at a fair distance (one place I lived had a pub the other side of the garden: very convenient but very noisy too!).

But even if you want a bit of space between you and the rowdy element, there's no getting away from the fact that it's inconvenient to live somewhere that doesn't have the right local facilities, and downright miserable in some circumstances. A case in point was the Christmas, a few years ago, when the car broke down, my husband was ill, and I needed a pharmacy. Trapped on a new suburban housing

Here's an idea for you... **Try a homefinder service. If you look on the internet (a Google search on 'homefinder' works) you'll get loads of names to choose from. As long as you can give them a sensible 'wish list' (semi-detached, three bedrooms, large garden, parking, nearby shops; cottage with roses round the door, pretty garden, near the sea) they'll find you a range of properties to consider.**

estate, with an ice-clad hill and nothing but a corner shop (and that a good twenty minutes away down a mud-track) I was helpless. My husband rolled in pain all day, while I swore that we'd move to somewhere where essential facilities were in easy reach.

What's on your 'essential' list? Start with the basics – mine includes (obviously) a pharmacist but I also want a few shops to browse, somewhere nice to eat and a bit of scenery. Then you need to think of the 'would like to have' facilities (like a decent theatre or a local cricket club). Don't even look at a property that doesn't include the basics, and make sure you're clear on what compromises you're making when you ignore things on the 'would like to have' list.

Defining idea... **'Love thy neighbour as yourself, but choose your neighbourhood.'**
LOUISE BEAL

But there's more to it than that, isn't there? How do you know what will suit you? If you've always lived in a city but fancy the seaside, or the countryside, how can you be sure that you'll be happy? I know a town dweller who spent a night in the country recently and nearly went mad with lack of sleep. Used to the traffic noise-pollution he still couldn't cope with the manic all-night song of the local nightingale.

If your chosen location's drastically different from anywhere else you've lived, book into a nearby hotel or holiday let for a few nights to get the feel of the place. Don't commit to move anywhere till you've covered the territory. No matter how attractive the place is, you can't tell whether it's going to be everything you want until you've had a really good look around the area at different times of the day, and on different days of the week. Drive around to see what facilities are nearby – is there a decent shopping centre? What's the traffic like at rush hour? Does the school down the road make life miserable for two half-hours every day when mothers drop off their kids?

Make sure you're prepared for seasonal variations too. Will it be hell in the bleak mid-winter? Is there an annual summer water shortage when the hordes of tourists arrive? It's also worth finding out about seasonal cost changes too. Life's no fun if your pint doubles in price every summer.

If it still looks OK, drill down to the detail. Walk the territory. Are the key facilities within easy reach? Look for a shop that sells basic groceries and newspapers, a doctor's and access to public transport.

**Kids objecting to the move? Your priorities have changed now, so next stop should be IDEA 30, *Kids' stuff*: it'll help you to sort out what's important.**

*Try another idea...*

*'Luck is being in the right place at the right time, but location and timing are to some extent under our control.'*
NATASHA JOSEFOWITZ, writer

*Defining idea...*

209

How did
it go?

**Q** **I'm torn. I've been looking for a smaller home in the area where I've always holidayed, and I've found two possibilities. One is near to most facilities but I'd love a good pub and there's nothing close. The other place has the pub – but the nearest shop is a car drive away. How do I choose?**

*A* *You've got two options: give up on both, since neither's what you want, and find a third place that fits the bill; alternatively you could try the old 'flip a coin' technique – which once helped me choose between two job offers. It sounds odd but, somehow, even though you know it's a trick, the gut-twist when you see how the coin's come down helps you understand where your heart really lies.*

**Q** **What's a good rule of thumb for deciding how accessible the facilities are?**

*A* *Before choosing a new home decide how far you are prepared to walk to essential facilities, and how far you are prepared to drive to those in the 'not essential' category. Get a good roadmap of the area and draw two circles around the property that's caught your eye. The inner circle is walking distance; the outer circle is easy-driving distance. Both distances depend on your own taste, but a general rule is that neither should take more than fifteen minutes to cover. Explore, marking the facilities you need on the map. If the vital ones are outside the inner circle, this property isn't for you.*

# 48

# Grandma Moses was seventy-five

**Just because you've had a lot of birthdays doesn't mean you've run out of bright ideas. In fact, what you lack in youth and energy you'll make up for in enthusiasm and experience. Give some thought to what inspires you and get creative.**

*It's true — Grandma Moses really was seventy-five when she began to paint in earnest.*

If I remember correctly she only started when she got too arthritic to carry on with her other hobbies, so she didn't sell her first painting till she was nearly eighty. And she's not the only example of someone who made a success with her creative ideas late in life. Think about Mary Wesley, whose first novel was published when she was seventy. There's nothing to stop you producing something wonderful, and I promise that even if you don't think you've a creative bone in your whole body you'll find something you can enjoy. Your only difficulty is deciding where your particular talent lies.

There you are, retired, plenty of time on your hands, enough cash to buy some materials. What takes your fancy? Paper, paint, wool, silk, canvas, glass, pottery...

Here's an idea for you...

**Invent a board game. No inspiration? Well, a London cabbie recently hit the jackpot with a game based on The Knowledge. What a great idea! Use your expertise to devise your own game. Once you've got your idea, don't waste it. You'll be doing your brain a huge favour by thinking through how the game will work and then making a prototype. User-test it with a few friends.**

The essence of creativity is that it comes from your own heart, so whatever you choose to do should be something that will give you immense satisfaction – not because you make a million with your first painting (though, naturally, that would be very pleasing) but because you can enjoy the process then stand back with pride and think 'I've created that.'

You don't have to follow any particular style, or form and you certainly don't have to follow any rules. Constable and Emin, Hirst and Da Vinci, Tolstoy and Rowling, Shakespeare and Poe – all artists, all successful, all different. You only have to be true to yourself, even if it turns out you're the only person who actually likes what you produce.

Defining idea...

*'I choose a block of marble and chop off whatever I don't need.'*
FRANÇOIS-AUGUSTE RODIN

And what might you produce? Go out and buy some wool and sew a tapestry, or knit a rainbow-coloured coat. Make bobbin lace or build a Queen Anne dolls' house. Produce a watercolour painting of your garden, or get your budgie to sit for a study in oils. Think texture, think colour, think shape. Or, if you've only ever produced knitting with large unsightly holes, if your doodle of a horse looks like a racing car, if you really can't see yourself creating anything that means using your hands, what about using your mind? Have you always thought you could write a novel, or are you longing to produce a book on the history of Tudor mushroom pickers? Or perhaps you're the kind of person who loves gadgets, and haunts those shops that sell things you never knew you needed? Do you have an idea for an invention that'll make our lives easier?

**If you don't feel creative but want a new hobby read IDEA 35, Oh. The paint's all dried up.**

*Try another idea...*

I think this part – where you're deciding what to produce – is crucial. There's such a lot of choice that it's really easy to get super-enthusiastic and start madly creating in three different directions. That's when you end up depressed – every morning the half-finished portrait of your lover glowers at you from the corner, the half-written novel piles on the guilt when you catch sight of your cluttered desk, and the unsewn silk and mohair dressing gown sheds miserably over the carpet.

But once you've made a choice that you're really enthusiastic about, you'll find that giving it your full attention, refining it, perfecting it, and actually finishing it is one of the best feelings in the world. Even if you don't manage to produce a masterpiece it's great fun having a go, just to see what you can do.

Incidentally, you don't have to spend a lot to get going and, really, perhaps you shouldn't until you're sure this is the medium for you.

*'A rock pile ceases to be a rock pile the moment a single man contemplates it, bearing within him the image of a cathedral.'*
ANTOINE DE SAINT-EXUPÉRY

*Defining idea...*

*How did it go?*

**Q**   **I think I've invented a new product but I don't have the ability to build a working prototype. I've got to have some help, but I'm worried my idea will get stolen if I ask for help. What's my next move?**

*A*   *You're right to be careful – why give your potential millions to some sharp entrepreneur who spots your good idea? I suggest you contact the Patents Office and find out how to get your idea protected.*

**Q**   **I've been painting for years and I could really do with raising some cash by selling some of them, but when I suggest it to my family they always laugh at me. Should I just give up and try something new?**

*A*   *The Turner prize is a perfect example of the rule that one man's art is another's poison. Take some of your paintings to a local gallery and get an opinion. If they laugh too, perhaps you'd better find another medium. On the other hand, you could be lucky.*

**Q**   **Have you got any suggestions that don't involve paint or fabric?**

*A*   *Try mosaics. Take those tiles left over from your various home improvement projects, and perhaps add a few extra for good luck (samples from shops are a good source). Then, depending on your mood or character, either smash them with a hammer (very therapeutic!), or cut them into neater pieces. Glue onto a surface, and grout. Try covering an old tabletop, or a paving-stone to create a small piece for the garden.*

# 49

# Life after death

**Dealing with the death of a person you love is the hardest thing you'll ever have to do, but believe me you will deal with it and rebuild your life. There is life after death: yours, and piecing it back together is by far the best way you can honour the memory of someone who loved you.**

*The worst thing about the death of someone you love is the fact that they're not there any more.*

I know that sounds obvious, but bereavement's a bit like having a baby – no matter how often people say 'It'll change your life', you don't really understand till the day you experience it for yourself.

The fact that a loved one is no longer a presence in this world is bewildering. When people walk out of your life there's always a kind of inner reassurance, just because you know the door isn't permanently closed – you might, one day, see them again. When they die there's this hole in your life that you know can't ever be filled. That realisation will be the first thing that you have to deal with and, I'm sorry to tell you, there's no easy way, no quick pain-relief trick. It sounds trite but the only real

Here's an idea for you...

**Walk down to your local florist to order your personal funeral wreath. Just standing amongst the flowers in the shop is a therapeutic activity.**

healer is time. In the meantime, your best bet is to bury yourself in the tons of practical issues you have to deal with. They may seem like the last thing you want to do but oddly they can help you cope with the sense of loss.

Notify friends and relatives. Be warned – this is always extremely difficult, and in the first few days it's a nightmare job, so make life easier on yourself and ask a friend or neighbour to phone half a dozen key people who can be asked to pass the news on further.

Find a funeral arranger. Most of them will take some of the burden off your shoulders – that's what they're there for – and they will certainly give you some advice on the various practicalities you're going to have to deal with. They'll book a date for the funeral and do much of the organising for you, but you will have to make some difficult choices so prepare to find the process exhausting.

Register the death at your local Registrar of Births and Deaths. This is a quick and easy process but is essential, or nothing else can happen, and you have a life to rebuild so there's no time to lose.

*Defining idea...*

*'Grief is the agony of an instant; the indulgence of grief the blunder of a life.'*
BENJAMIN DISRAELI

If you're having some kind of service you will, at some point, be asked to give some personal details, choose appropriate readings and music so think about what you would like.

If there are financial issues to be sorted (and there usually are) speak to the executors, or to your solicitor so that the legal process – and practical matters like notifying pension providers and banks – can be put in hand quickly.

The day of a loved one's funeral is hideous but at least you're doing something and have people around you. In my experience, the day after is worse. Whatever you do, don't sit around doing nothing. Do something you enjoy, even if it's something very tiny. Have your hair done; have a facial; play a round of golf; go into town and buy yourself a cream cake: do anything that will give you time to be 'you', and will help you get started on your new life. Don't feel guilty about this. Your life has to go on – your partner wouldn't have wanted it any other way.

**When you've lost someone you love it's sometimes hard to let go. For some ideas on how to pick yourself up again, read IDEA 33, *Feeling blue?***

*Try another idea...*

**'Strength is born in the deep silence of long-suffering hearts; not amid joy.'**
FELICIA HEMANS, poet

*Defining idea...*

217

*How did it go?*

**Q**  **My husband died eleven months ago. I cry every day, and I can't bear to clear out his clothes – it feels as though I'm betraying him. Friends have suggested I see a counsellor, but I don't want to talk about it. Should I? How long does grief take?**

*A*  *I'm sorry to sound so cruel, but grief won't go away if you don't allow it to. It's like a nagging tooth – your tongue insists on probing just so you can reassure yourself that it's still hurting. You're holding on to your grief and you need to start letting it go. Please, do go to see the counsellor, and while you're there, get one of your friends to clear out the wardrobe so you can come back and begin to live your life again. You ask how long grief takes. The Victorians had some logic in their year of mourning, because the first anniversary of any death is really hard to deal with. After that, as long as you allow it to happen, the grief does then begin to ease and is replaced by loving memories.*

**Q**  **I've met someone new and want to marry her, but my family are outraged because it's so soon after my first wife's death. Do you think I should wait?**

*A*  *If it's been much less than a year since your wife died, I'd advise you to wait a little before you remarry, not because of public opinion but simply because I reckon you need to feel comfortable as a single person again before you become part of another couple. That doesn't mean, of course, that you can't fall in love again – it's not something you have much choice about, is it? Just take it steady.*

## 50

# Lawn today, lawn tomorrow

**It'll still be there. Still needing cutting, raking, weeding, seeding and feeding. Are you a lifelong non-gardener? Do you have a field outside the front door? Plant the kind of garden that works for you.**

If you're looking with loathing at the scrubland outside your window ('You've got time to do something about that garden now you're retired, haven't you dear?'), here's how to make life easy.

Draw a rough plan of your garden with a wiggly line dividing it into two, fairly equal, halves. Choose one half to be the bit where you can sit and relax. The other half's going to be the bit to look at while you're guzzling beer/sipping shiraz (delete as applicable).

*Here's an idea for you...*

For a low-maintenance garden with a bit of excitement lay slabs, or some other stone, over most of your plot, leaving just a couple of small corners for plants. These can be simple flower beds, pretty tubs, or even raised beds if that suits you better. Don't, whatever you do, go for run-of-the-mill stuff (and especially not geraniums, busy lizzies, or begonias because they just don't cut it). Go for something a bit exotic, like orchids, bonsai trees or carnivorous plants.

## THE SITTING AND RELAXING BIT

Perfect lawns are hard work – I once saw a friend hissing angrily over a reckless leaf that had dared to land on his lush velvet grass. However, if you're like me – happy as long as there's a hint of green (what's wrong with clover for goodness' sake?) –they're cheap, and it's lovely to laze on the lawn on a hot day. When spring arrives, soak the scrubland with weed killer, marinate well, rotavate, rake, then lay turf green-side-up. Leave it a few weeks to settle and you'll be on the sunlounger by summertime.

Slabs or stone blocks are more backbreaking and more expensive to lay than grass but, on the upside, all you need to maintain them is a broom.

Gravel. Hmm, I've got mixed feelings. Raked into Japanese swirls it's very zen; but forget it unless you enjoy cleaning up cat poop.

If you fancy camomile, get plants that are guaranteed weed-free. We spent hours fighting tiny moss-like invaders but eventually they beat us and we said a reluctant farewell to the truly fabulous scented lawn. Oh, and by the way, you have to plant each baby camomile plant by hand, so either throw a planting party or make an advance booking with your osteopath.

Decking is still depressingly popular. OK it's cheap and easy to lay, but I've never understood why it's laid in damp England, where it gets slimy and needs resealing every year.

**IDEA 37, *Planes, trains and free travel passes*, might just help you get away from the jungle.**

*Try another idea...*

Finally, a wild meadow sounds perfect for the lazy gardener – romantic, environmentally friendly, low maintenance – but it takes forever to establish and you'll need to do some serious research before you begin, so it's not quite as lazy an option as it sounds!

## THE SOMETHING TO LOOK AT BIT

Don't be fooled by all that crap about micro-climate, aspect and soil type. Use common sense (don't put desert plants in a bog garden) and most plants grow anywhere – check your neighbours' gardens to see what does well. If you plant one or two that don't thrive, dig 'em up and plant something else. Here's the lazy-woman's guide.

The easiest option is a mix of mostly shrubs, a few perennials and some bulbs. Prune the shrubs occasionally and tidy the perennials; most bulbs flower happily year after year without any attention. Chuck a bit of plant food over it all occasionally. You can include roses too – just prune them every spring and spray them with rose fertilizer and bug killer

'**The grass is not, in fact, always greener on the other side of the fence. Fences have nothing to do with it. The grass is greenest where it is watered.**'
ROBERT FULGHUM, writer and polymath

*Defining idea...*

twice a year. Mind you, if you fancy an entire rose garden you'll need to put something down to stop weeds growing between the plants. The occasional tree is OK but be warned, they always end up *bigger* than the label suggests.

On no account leave out the shrubs and plant an entire herbaceous border or a cottage garden or, even worse, a vegetable patch. You won't believe how much work you'll have to do to keep these looking perfect.

Annuals, usually in day-glo colours, get planted out in late spring and need devoted attention all summer. Hard work and uncool.

In contrast, a few evergreen plants in pots do look rather cool. They're relatively easy to maintain but need watering in summer. If you have more than ten pots and don't put in an automatic watering system, here are my friend's standard instructions for her garden-sitter:

- Open bottle of wine.

- Pour first glass of wine and begin drinking.

- Start watering pots.

- Continue watering plants until bottle is empty.

**Q**   **I love my garden as it is, but you've got me thinking about the future, when I might not be able to look after all this. Should I change it now?**

*A*   *That would be a shame. You might stay fit enough to look after the garden for decades yet. Why don't you put some money to one side so you can employ a gardener if you ever need to?*

**Q**   **I like the idea of becoming an expert, but only if I can get a bit of a kick out of showing my plants. How do I go about that?**

*A*   *The best idea is to find a society that specialises in your plant of choice. There's bound to be one: try asking in your local library, or looking on the internet.*

**Q**   **Now I'm around the house more, I'm thinking off fulfilling a long-held dream of keeping chickens. Is this a good idea?**

*A*   *A great idea in principle. A couple of chickens wandering around add a soothing air of rural tranquillity to even the most suburban of gardens. And your own eggs will taste better than anything you can buy from a supermarket. The drawbacks? They need a certain amount of daily maintenance (who will do this while you're taking your long holidays?). They need somewhere safe (i.e. fox proof) to sleep at night, so you'll have to buy or build a house for them. They will eat the fresh green bits of your precious plants, and turn your lawn into guano field – though you will have the best compost in the neighbourhood.*

How did it go?

223

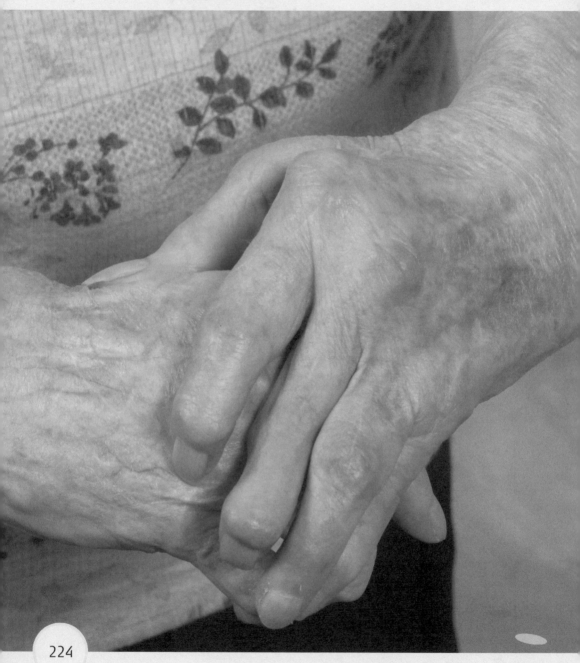

# My arm isn't long enough

**If you can't hold the paper far enough away to be able to read it, you're already familiar with the joys of long-sightedness. Nature has lots of weird little surprises in store as all sorts of bits take turns to grumble, or simply go on strike. Here are a few little tips for dealing with new-found physical limitations.**

*A sense of humour certainly helps with the minor irritants.*

I've got arthritis in my little toe, and part of my morning routine is clicking the joint back into place. Yes, I know it's hilarious, but at the same time it hurts like hell (OK, only for a split second). Still, I can't imagine what it must be like to have constant, serious pain. If you're already suffering from any of the worst diseases associated with ageing, there are three routes to helping yourself cope.

**HEALTH**

Obviously you'll get help from your doctor (you have seen your doctor haven't you? If not, then get thee to a physician pronto – why suffer alone?) but there are some simple things you can do to improve your general health.

Here's an idea for you... **If your hearing loss isn't treatable, for goodness' sake get a hearing aid. They're tiny these days and we'll all be very grateful that we don't have to repeat everything twice. The latest models are expensive, but it's money well spent.**

If you feel lousy, it's desperately tempting to spend the days eating nice food and relaxing in front of the box, but in the long run this just makes everything worse. Read up on pretty well any disease associated with ageing and you'll find the things that make it worse include obesity, high blood pressure, lack of exercise, poor diet, smoking and high cholesterol. In short, it's really important to eat a healthy diet, keep fit and deal with the bad habits.

## ATTITUDE

We all know a few people who seem to enjoy their disease and others who just hide their head in the sand pretending it's not happening, but I contend it's better to face up to the truth. If you admit you have a problem and then spend a bit of time finding out about it – easily done via library or internet – you can do a lot to supplement your general healthcare.

Take arthritis, for example. I'm rather horrified to find that a daily dose of cod liver oil helps to lubricate all the joints. I always thought that was just something that stern Victorian parents handed out to kids to punish them for being young. You'll already know that you need to rest, but keep as fit as you can, too. It's grim to get up and move about when you're in pain, but if you give in to this disease you'll seize up like the tin man in the *Wizard of Oz*.

Failing eyesight – glaucoma, cataracts, macular degeneration (the most common cause of loss of vision loss among the over sixties) – there may be no pain so the one, crucial step you can take is to have your eyes tested regularly.

**So you think you're too disabled to be creative? Take some inspiration from IDEA 48, *Grandma Moses was seventy-five* (and she had arthritis too!).**

*Try another idea...*

Hearing loss. Hmm. I get the distinct impression some of my aged relatives see this as a mixed blessing. While it irritates them that they can't always catch the conversation, I'm convinced they like being able to ignore things they don't want to hear. If you spent your entire youth at Hawkwind concerts you may still have ringing in the ears and I'm afraid you're stuck with it, but if your ears are good, try not to jeopardise them by subjecting them to prolonged overloud noise.

Gum disease – eminently avoidable and worth sorting out for the sake of yourself and everyone else (you may even get lucky romantically once your mouth's fresh again). Go to the dentist and take his advice!

## LIFESTYLE

Where do I start? There are loads of clever aids available. Check out your local council, read some of the thousand or so catalogues that come through the letterbox every day with offers of all the things you never knew you needed. Visit your local shop for the disabled – even if you don't consider yourself 'disabled' it doesn't mean you can't take advantage of the gadgets they stock.

*'Crises and deadlocks when they occur have at least this advantage, that they force us to think.'*
JAWAHARLAL NEHRU

*Defining idea...*

227

*How did it go?*

**Q** **I do my best to stay fit and healthy but I'm in so much pain! Is there any other way I can make my life easier?**

*A* *I don't think our society takes chronic pain seriously enough – there seems to be a general attitude of 'you'll just have to put up with it'. I don't agree. First talk to your doctor and insist that you're given the right treatment to control your pain and then consider some of the complementary pain control ideas. I can't tell you what'll work for you but heat pads, acupuncture, acupressure, relaxation and meditation are all helpful for pain relief. Just a word of warning though – if you go for any complementary medicines, check with your doctor to make sure they won't react with your prescription medication.*

**Q** **There are so many small things that give me trouble. How can I deal with all these tribulations?**

*A* *Lateral-think your way around difficulties. For example, if you can't open jam jars, you could: get a neighbour to open them; pay a schoolchild to open them every weekend; buy a jar-opening gadget; smash the jars on the floor and scrape up the contents (silly I grant you, but it reminds me that a sharp tap sometimes loosens lids); make your own jam; buy home-made jam, with a paper cover; buy tarts and scrape the jam off. Yes another silly one, but it leads to: get one of those plunger things used to put jam in doughnuts and have a neighbour fill it every so often from a new jar.*

# First amongst equals

**Sometimes it's difficult to decide where your priorities lie, particularly if you're busy. Brush up your time management skills for a more enjoyable retirement.**

Some people are always rushing around in headless chicken mode.

If you're one of them – forever fire fighting, always running late, feeling rushed and overburdened, retirement should be the answer. But is it? If you've always worked this way you may be appalled to find in a month or so that you're in exactly the same boat, having merely exchanged one set of pressures for another.

If this is you, let me suggest there must be a benefit to all this time pressure or you wouldn't put yourself through it. What do you get out of being this busy? Does the feeling of being in demand give you a kick? Or perhaps you don't think anyone else can do the job as well as you can? Or you could be like my husband, who desperately hurtles around the house and garden trying to make them perfect, simply because he's avoiding getting down to the work he has to finish by next week. (Another neat avoidance trick he uses is to keep his desk in total chaos, so he always has to spend half an hour finding the particular papers he needs to begin work.)

Here's an idea for you...

**List the rooms in your home, and by each write the principal jobs that need to be done there. Now start with one room and do just the jobs you've written down. Don't do anything else that occurs to you as you go, and don't move on to another room until this one is finished.**

Let's look at the main causes of time pressure, and how to deal with them.

Occasionally you'll be genuinely pushing up against a near-impossible deadline because there's genuinely too much to do, that can only be done by you. You've got too little time to do it and the deadline can't be extended. If this is you at the moment, that's OK as long as it's short term (but be warned – constant stress at this level is unhealthy). Get on with it, push the adrenalin around and feel satisfied when you're done. But if you've been like it for months or, worse, for most of your life, I have to tell you that you're not genuinely time pressured.

It could just be that you're disorganised. The desk, the house, the car, all are chaotic. Socks are pulled out from the dirty linen basket to be worn again if they pass the sniff test, papers float around the desk in a constant maelstrom, nothing can ever be found without a frantic search through the clutter. The answer to this is pretty obvious isn't it? Take a day out and tidy up. From there on, keep it tidy. Touch each piece of paper once. Deal with it; file it away in a cabinet (not in a pile on the floor). Do the washing before the basket's full (ditto the ironing, if you can bear it – though I have no right to preach about that particular chore). Clean as you go, rather than leaving it all till chaos reigns again.

Defining idea...

*'The harder you work, the harder it is to surrender.'*
VINCE LOMBARDI, American football coach

Although it always takes me ages to convince the disorganised that they must take the time out to organise themselves, they always see the benefit once they've done it.

Now you've sorted out your priorities, get things moving with IDEA 16, *Earplugs at the ready?***

Try another idea...

Maybe you're a sucker? This is either because you're soft hearted, kind and loving, or because you're terrified of what people will think of you if you say no to some unreasonable request (or even some reasonable request that's just the final straw on your looming haystack of tasks). Learn to say it. Practice the words: 'No, I'm too busy at the moment.' I know it's hard, but the odds are that these people will soon find someone else to do it – and they may even respect you for finally standing your ground.

Or maybe you're a perfectionist? Sorry, but nothing's perfect – and perfection would be really boring. It's our imperfections that make us human and interesting.

The White Rabbit put on his spectacles. 'Where shall I begin, please your Majesty?' he asked. 'Begin at the beginning,' the King said, very gravely, 'and go on till you come to the end; then stop.'
LEWIS CARROLL, *Alice's Adventures in Wonderland*

Defining idea...

*How did it go?*

**Q   I'm a terrible procrastinator, particularly with things I don't really want to do. I keep putting them off and, of course, they turn into crises? Any tips?**

A   *The first thing to do is to work out what exactly is stopping you from doing these various things. Are you bored? Are they too difficult? Too easy? Then decide what's the upside for getting the job done and focus hard on that. There's no reason why every task has to be fun, but as long as the result is worth the effort even a boring task can be tackled.*

**Q   I'm always rushed because of other people's demands on my time, but I don't know how to get out of my commitments.**

A   *You may be needed by other people, but if you're pushing yourself too hard you risk making yourself ill with stress – and then they'll have to do without you entirely. Set some boundaries with them; make them understand that some times are for you alone.*

**Q   How can I manage my time better?**

A   *Keep a time log for a week to find out why you're always rushed. It's a bit of a fag, but well worth the effort. Use a small notebook that you can keep with you, dividing each page into three columns. Head column 1 'activity', column 2 'time', and column 3 'review'. Every hour (yes, I said it was a fag) note what you've been doing and for how long. Every evening fill in the third column. Was it worth doing? What didn't you do because you were doing it? At the end of the week, review everything. Where are you spending most of your time? Where are you wasting time?*

# The end...

Or is it a new beginning?

We hope that the ideas in this book will have inspired you to try new things, given you an insight into what retirement is really all about and made you realise that what you can do with your life after work is almost without limit.

So, why not let *us* know how you got on? What did it for you – what new interests have you developed, what fantastic places have you visited and what do you plan to do next? Maybe you've got some tips of your own that you'd like to share. If you liked this book you may find we have more brilliant ideas for other areas that could help change your life for the better. You'll find us, and a host of other brilliant ideas, online at www.infideas.com.

If you prefer to write, then send your letters to:
*Enjoy retirement*
The Infinite Ideas Company Ltd
36 St Giles, Oxford OX1 3LD, United Kingdom

We want to know what you think, because we're all working on making our lives better too. Give us your feedback and you could win a copy of another *52 Brilliant Ideas* book of your choice. Or maybe get a crack at writing your own.

Good luck. Be brilliant.

# Offer one

## CASH IN YOUR IDEAS

We hope you enjoy this book. We hope it inspires, amuses, educates and entertains you. But we don't assume that you're a novice, or that this is the first book that you've bought on the subject. You've got ideas of your own. Maybe our author has missed an idea that you use successfully. If so, why not send it to yourauthormissedatrick@infideas.com, and if we like it we'll post it on our bulletin board. Better still, if your idea makes it into print we'll send you four books of your choice or the cash equivalent. You'll be fully credited so that everyone knows you've had another Brilliant Idea.

# Offer two

## HOW COULD YOU REFUSE?

Amazing discounts on bulk quantities of Infinite Ideas books are available to corporations, professional associations and other organisations.

For details call us on:
+44 (0)1865 514888
Fax: +44 (0)1865 514777
or e-mail: info@infideas.com

# Where it's at...

ageism 59–62
althernative therapies 139
    Alexander Technique 140
    aromatherapy 140
    martial arts 142
    meditation 141
    reflexology 140–1
    tai chi 141
anxiety 53–7
assertiveness 88–9
    fogging 90
    PLAN 89
attitude 59–60
    positive 62
    start a passive revolution
        60–1, 62

beauty regimes 29–30
    cosmetic surgery 32, 33
    face shaping 31
    make-up 30–1, 33
    see also grooming
blushing 57

care
    animals 162
    caring for someone else 161
    equipment 162
    home care 160, 162

nursing homes 161
sheltered housing 159
someone else's home 161
children
    communicating with 134
    don't be a burden 133
    don't be taken for granted 133
    learn to say no 134
    looking after 131–2
    upsetting 134
clothes 117–18
    accessories 119
    appropriate 118
    how to choose 151–2
    mother-of-the-bride rule 150
    mutton and lamb rule 150
    personal stylist 153
    style 149, 153
    trendy 153
creativity 211–13
    protecting ideas 214
    selling 214
crime
    household prevention 43–4, 46
    personal prevention 44–5, 46

daredevil sports 5–8
death 215
    funerals 216–17

grief 218
practical issues 216
re-marriage 218
decorating 73–6
dependence
    emergency state 204
    encourage independence 204
    helping others 206
    long-term 204
    loss of confidence 205
    pseudo-dependency 204
    slide into helplessness 203
depression
    clinical 144
    feeling blue 143–4
    get rid of the emotion 147
    symptoms 145–6
    treatment 146
diet 47–8
    advice 110
    alcohol 51
    calories 48
    health problems 112
    MUM plan 49–50, 51
    portion size 48
    right nutrients 111
    Variety Diet 111, 112
    way of life 48
doctors 7, 8, 83, 142

experience, writing about 4

finance
delayed access savings 195
instant access cash 194
long-term investments 196
property 197
savings 193, 197
fitness 83–4
check 84–5
tips 85, 86
freedom 135
friends 99
be interested 100, 101
finding love 102
join a club 100
opening lines 100–1
re-finding 191
fun 25–8, 136
funerals 42, 216–17

gadgets
finding 201, 202
necessary 200
unneccessary 200
gardens 219
changing 223
sitting and relaxing 220–1
something to look at 221–2
goals 69
action planning 71
line up resources 70
Plan B 72

realising dreams 136–8
smart 70–1, 72
spot the blockers 69–70
time-out progress check
185–8
grooming 91–2
baldness 93
body 93
cleanse, tone, moisturise 92
cost 94
facials 92
hair 93
hands and feet 93, 94
liver spots 93
male 94
see also beauty regimes

health
arthritis 116
attitude 226–7
chronic pain 228
eyesight 116
gum disease 116
hearing 116
lifestyle 116
looking after 226
minor irritants 224, 228
psychosomatic disorders 171
regular checks 181
relax 170
screening 182–4
spa breaks 170, 171
symptoms of illness 167–8

visit the doctor 169, 171
wait a couple of weeks 169
health checkups 7, 8
hobbies 14
holidays 35–8
with friends 38
house swaps 36, 38
planning 36–7
timeshares 38
household chores 15, 16

income 17
budgets 17–18
buy household items 19
debts 18, 20
limited 199
independent financial advisers 81
inner demons 53–7
invisibility 87–8

jobs
become a guru 180
CVs 11, 12
giving advice 180
interviews 11, 12
occupation description 177–9
searching 9–12

leisure pursuits
discard never-used equipment
155–6
investigate 157
make lists 156

prioritise 157
set challenges 158
time allocation 157
living in the present 2–4, 130
location for living 207–8
    basic facilities 208
    choosing 210
    rule of thumb 210
    trial run 209
    walk the territory 209
love 102

meditation 67, 141
mental health 121–2
    create targets 123
    do something different 122–3
    learn something new 125
    memory joggers 123–4
    take a degree 125

partners 13–16
pensions
    annuities 80
    benefits 79
    early retirement 79, 81
    increasing 79
    independent financial advice
        81
    private 79
    state 77–8
    tax-free lump sum 81

personal space 14, 16
phobias 53
problem solving 127
    don't procrastinate 128
    live for the moment 130
    multi-tasking 129
    prioritise 128
    schedule 'me time' 130
    stop worrying 128–9

reflect on plans 185–8
relationships, rekindling 189–92
reminiscence 1–4
risk-taking 5–8

sex 21–2
    men 22–3
    starting and experimenting
        24
    women 23
smoking 173–6
social life 15
    cliques 98
    local activities 95–6
    set up own group 97, 98
space 105
    creating 108
    negotiating 106
    planning 106–7
stereotypes 117–18
    changing 120

clothes 117–19
keep up to date 120
moods and attitudes 119
stress 63
    common symptoms 64
    fight or flight reaction 64
    get help 65
    handling 115
    health 116
    learn to accept situation 66
    meditate 67
    personality type 114
    preventing 114
    prioritise 66
    reactions 113–14

time pressure 229–30
    causes of/dealing with 230–1
    managing 232
    procrastination 232
travel insurance 8
travel and transport 163–4
    cars 164–5, 166
    driving tests 16
    local network 164

wills
    financial provisions 41
    making 39–41
    sort papers 41

# Here's YOUR chance to win!

## Complete the wordsearch for an opportunity to win £5,000!

```
U N E H C T I K R G
J S V T C W N G E O
T C A M E R A K T L
C I S H L O C K U D
R H C V O M R R P W
U O J K C L J K M A
I O L U E D I G O T
S C A S H T H D C C
E H N V H M S R A H
S P O R T S C A R Y
```

Left are ten prizes won recently in consumer competitions. All you have to do is find them and ring them in the wordsearch panel. They may read right to left, left to right, up, down or diagonally. But – one won't be found!

**Simply write down the missing prize in the coupon below and post today – and the £5,000 could be yours!**

GOLDWATCH
SPORTSCAR
CASH

COMPUTER
KITCHEN
CRUISE
CAMERA

JEWELLERY
TICKETS
USAHOLIDAY

---

To be in with a chance of winning **£5,000**, simply cut out this voucher and mail it to: Accolade Publishing, 800 Guillat Avenue, Kent Science Park, Sittingbourne, ME9 8GU

The 'missing prize' is.................................................................

Name.........................................................................................

Address.....................................................................................

.................................................................................................

.................................................................................................

.................................................Postcode ...............................

Telephone.................................................................................

Email.........................................................................................

Promotional code ER0706

# Make your retirement a winning move

Take out a subscription to any one of these **Accolade Publishing** newsletters with an exclusive **20% discount** and you could win fantastic prizes. Accolade are experts in making people winners, providing thousands of winning opportunities to readers every month.

**You can claim your discount by calling 0870 428 7949 to subscribe and quoting promotional code 'IFER0706'**

## Competitor's Companion

Includes full details of every consumer competition in the country worth winning and provides everything you need to enter. So you no longer have to hunt around to reap the rewards of lots of competition wins. You could be spending your retirement winning cars, going on holidays of a lifetime and even treating the family.

**Claim your 20% discount and pay just £47.50 for a 12 month subscription (Usual price £59.40)**

## Everyone's a Winner

Jam-packed with puzzles including word searches, crosswords, number problems and word games. And what's even better is that with each puzzle there is a prize up for grabs exclusively to *Everyone's a Winner* readers, increasing your chances of winning. Prizes include holidays in the sun, weekend breaks and electrical items for your home!

**Claim your 20% discount and pay just £55.20 for a 12 month subscription (Usual price £69.00)**

## Quiz Winner

A monthly magazine dedicated to quizzing. Every issue is packed with quizzes to play and great prizes to win. It also features quizzing news, takes you behind the scenes of major TV quiz shows and interviews the winners! You'll find out how to get on quiz shows yourself and how to boost your memory of trivia to help you win.

**Claim your 20% discount and pay just £55.20 for a 12 month subscription (Usual price £69.00)**

To read some winning testimonials, find out more about the newsletters or to see the types of prizes you could be winning visit www.accoladepublishing.co.uk or call 0870 428 7949 for more details.

Acc lade
Publishing Ltd